S0-BBQ-169

The Wisdom of Bishop Sheen

"The supreme dignity of the human person, which is the foundation of democracy, is also the foundation of courtesy . . ."

"It is the things that we like that make our character."

"Habits which make a man wise do not necessarily make a man good. Intellectual habits will make a man a good violinist, but will not make him moral."

"The pure can look on the impure without contempt."

"The souls of men are tried less by work than by the frustration that comes from too much attention to the trivial."

"He who thinks he has done enough has done nothing."

"Rest never seems to be where we are, but other-where. Then when we get there, it seems to have gone somewhere else."

Way to Happy Living

BY FULTON J. SHEEN

A Fawcett Crest Book

FAWCETT PUBLICATIONS, INC., GREENWICH, CONN.
MEMBER OF AMERICAN BOOK PUBLISHERS COUNCIL, INC.

Nihil Obstat: John M. A. Fearns, S.T.D.,
Censor Librorum.

Imprimatur: ✠ Francis Cardinal Spellman,
Archbishop of New York.
July 26, 1955

The nihil obstat and imprimatur are official declarations
that a book or pamphlet is free of doctrinal or moral error.
No implication is contained therein that those who have
granted the nihil obstat and imprimatur agree with the
contents, opinions or statements expressed.

A Fawcett Crest Book reprinted by arrangement with
the George Matthew Adams Service.

This book contains the complete text of the
original hardcover edition.

Copyright 1955 by Maco Magazine Corporation.
All rights reserved, including the right to reproduce
this book or portions thereof.

Second Fawcett Crest printing, March 1966

Published by Fawcett World Library,
67 West 44th Street, New York, New York 10036.
Printed in the United States of America.

CONTENTS

Part V: Character

Part VI: Forgiveness

Part VII: Humility

Part VIII: Sorrow

Part IX: Communication

*Way to
Happy Living*

HAPPINESS

CHAPTER ONE

Does Happiness Consist in Riches?

THERE IS NO ONE who does not want to be happy. To seek happiness is a proof of our imperfection. As Pascal expressed it: "All men have happiness as their object: there is no exception. However different the means they employ, they all aim at the same end."

"O happiness! our being's end and aim,
Good, pleasure, ease, content! whate'er they name,
  That something still which prompt th' eternal sigh,
For which we bear to live, or dare or die."
(Alexander Pope)

Nor do we want this happiness through another man's eyes; we want it as something peculiarly our own. The difficulty is where to find it. The fact that we feel happy when we receive something we want, and that we feel unhappy when we are deprived of it, proves that happiness has something to do with the objects of our desires or purposes. For that reason, at the end of every human activity there are pleasure and joy or sadness and pain, just as at the end of every human life there is a heaven or a hell.

Does happiness consist of riches or wealth? There are indeed many advantages to riches. Herodotus claimed that they allowed a man to indulge his passions. George Bernard Shaw said that money gave power: "Money talks; money prints; money broadcasts; money reigns." But wealth can never constitute happiness, because it is only a means to happiness and extrinsic to oneself. This is what Our Lord meant when He said, "A man's life does not consist in the abundance of his possessions." If you put a penny close enough to your eye, you can shut out the light of the sun. Want of wealth is not necessarily the cause of unhappiness. There are more divorces, more frustrated lives, more inner misery among the rich than among the poor. "A golden bit does not make the better horse."

Riches in great abundance have a peculiar quality; they make men more greedy. As Thomas Jefferson said, "I have not observed men's honesty to increase with their riches." No matter how much money a rich man has, he hates to lose what he has, just as no matter how many hairs he has on his head, it hurts to have one pulled out. This spirit of covetousness hardens the soul, and drew from Our Divine Lord the warning: "It is easier for a camel to pass through the eye of a needle, than for a rich man to enter the Kingdom of God." "But woe to you rich! for you are now having your comfort."

There is a peculiar paradox about riches: the more covetous the rich man is, the poorer he is, for there is always something he wants. But the consecrated souls who have taken the vow of poverty are richer than all the rich, for there is nothing they desire; therefore they possess everything.

In any case, how foolish to make happiness consist in that which one day we must leave. If riches are really ours, why can we not take them with us? The only things we can carry with us at death are what we might carry away in a shipwreck. As Shakespeare said: "If thou art rich, thou art poor; for like an ass whose back with ingots bows, thou bearest thy heavy riches but a journey and death unloads thee." On the last day, relatives and friends will gather around the death-bed of the rich man and ask: "How much did he leave?" for wherever there is a will, there is a lawsuit. But the angels will ask: "How much did he take with him?" "The land of a certain rich man brought forth abundant crops. And he began to take thought within himself, saying, 'What shall I do, for I have no room to store my crops?' And he said, 'I will do this: I will pull down my barns and build larger ones, and there I will store up all my grain and my goods. And I will say to my soul: Soul, thou hast many good things laid up for many years; take thy ease—eat, drink, be merry.' But God said to him, 'Thou fool, this night do they demand thy soul of thee; and the things that thou has provided, whose will they be?' So is he who lays up treasure for himself, and is not rich as regards God."

CHAPTER TWO

Does Happiness Consist in Glory, Reputation and Honors?

REPUTATION AND HONORS are witnesses to excellence or prominence, but they do not constitute it. Making honor the goal of life is to make our happiness dependent upon others, and happiness should be something no one can take away. Furthermore, if honor is the ideal of life, then disgrace is the only sin.

It is really not honor based on virtue which men seek today, but rather reputation, which is measured more by its width than its depth. Reputation is often only popularity, and, like a breeze, it cannot be kept. You must enjoy it while it blows. It is like a ball—men generally start kicking it about when it stops rolling. The greatness of any age is to be measured by those whom it holds in high repute. The youth of today is not in danger because of its love of pleasures, but because it worships the wrong kind of heroes. Many of the present century who have reputations will be quoted in the next century to prove how barbarous was the thinking of this century.

Anyone who enjoys the world's repute, if he is hon-

est with himself, knows that he does not deserve it.
The world is either saying things about us that are
too good to be true, or too bad to be true. As Charles
Lamb put it: "I am accounted by some people a
good man. How cheap that character is acquired! Pay
your debts, don't borrow money, nor twist your kit-
ten's neck off, nor disturb a congregation, etc.; your
business is done. I know things about myself, which
would make every friend fly me as a plague." St.
Philip Neri, seeing a condemned man led to the guil-
lotine, said: "There goes Philip Neri, except for the
grace of God."

How unstable is happiness based on "being well
known"! How many go up like sky-rockets and come
down like sticks! Applause is contagious. Let two or
three applaud in a theatre and everyone follows. As
Shakespeare said:

"Glory is like a circle in the water,

Which never ceaseth to enlarge itself

Till, by broad spreading, it disperse to nought."

The truly happy person does not really care what
others may think of him, for true glory consists in
the judgment of God rather than in the judgment of
men. St. Paul said: "It is a very small matter to be
judged by you or by man's tribunal." The most last-
ing reputations are those that are achieved after death
when the tinsel of empty glory fades away. The greatness of Lincoln is posthumous. The glory of Christ
came after His Crucifixion. And from Him has come
this warning: "Woe to you when all men speak well
of you."

No stronger words escaped the Divine Lips than
those directed against popularity-seekers, who sought
to have their names publicized in the market places
then, as they do today in the newspapers: "All their

CHAPTER THREE

Happiness

HAPPINESS does not consist in the abundance of things a man possesses, nor does it reside in the satisfaction of different specific desires—for example, pleasure at one moment, publicity at another. Rather, happiness is conditioned on two things: an over-all purpose in life and, second, the crushing of egotism and selfishness.

The goal of life must satisfy the highest reaches of personality, namely our desire for life, our craving for truth, and our lust for love. Life is not satisfied by three more days of living, but by unending immortality; truth is satisfied, not by knowing all geography to the exclusion of science, or all art to the exclusion of philosophy; the mind can come to rest only when it possesses a knowledge of all truth, not in an abstract form, but personalized in Him Who says: "I am the Truth." Finally, the will is satisfied not by a love that grows cold or has phases like the moon, but by a love that is a continuous ecstasy without hate or satiety. This Perfect Life, Perfect Truth and Perfect Love is God, Father, Son and Holy Spirit.

The second condition of happiness is crushing

egotism and selfishness which stands in the way of attaining that ultimate goal or purpose. Hell is the ego affirmed in time, in isolation and in eternity in conflict with other egos who are constantly negating our ego. Hell is composed of completely egotistic persons! Those who presently live with such people now have a foretaste of hell. The reason the ego has to be naughted is because unless a ''for sale'' sign is hung on it, neither God nor neighbor can move in. Only when the glass tube has had all the air removed and becomes a vacuum, can it become the medium for X-rays which can penetrate the flesh and brain though we see it not. So long as there remains the ego or selfishness by which we affirm our pleasure over others, we are consumed by an inner unhappiness. In hell, nothing burns but the ego—a sensation that egotists dimly feel in the gnawing that goes on inside their conscience.

Because it is so hard to get rid of pride and lust, covetousness and anger, gluttony and sloth, the business of achieving happiness below is very slow. Inner peace is rarely attained in one stroke; we have to inch ourselves through the door of happiness. There are no plains in the spiritual life. We do not just climb a few paces through rough roads and then finally come to a land of contentment. Rather, we reach only a momentary clearing; the brushes, thorns and briars still lie ahead to cut and bruise the flesh; the occasional danger of slipping back a few feet now and then is ever present. As Our Divine Lord said: ''Take up your cross daily.'' The struggle for happiness is even conditioned upon having a wrestling match with ourselves; it is not easy to get the lion and the lamb to lie down together; the retriever has a hard time catching his quarry, the wild beast within us; if it does happen, it is by the skin of one's teeth.

But even though it be difficult, there is a peace and a joy about the pursuit of Divine Happiness which the egotist cannot understand. Each trial and struggle has its strength as grace pours in from heaven above. The more the balloon of our egotism is shot full of holes, the more apertures are made for the influx of light and love. Our own individual resources never have to be budgeted against the daily crosses. Others wonder whence come strength and patience, never suspecting that such souls are no longer self-contained cisterns that quickly run dry; rather they are great reservoirs into which the sluice gates of heaven open. Everybody wants to be happy. The reason most people are not happy is because they want to be happy in their own way and without any purchase price. Paradoxical as it may seem, happiness begins when the ego dies.

CHAPTER FOUR

Pleasures

PLEASURE is very peculiar: to possess it one must not seek it directly, but rather seek it through something else. Not even an avid cocktail drinker takes a cocktail to have pleasure, rather, he has pleasure because he takes a cocktail. Pleasure does not cause itself, but is caused by the possession of some good or the attainment of some purpose.

Our complex modern society is directed to the creation of mass pleasure rather than individual pleasure. Movies, television, advertising are geared to the masses, and generally to their lowest common denominator. Their aim is to satisfy what men have in common, rather than what they have individually. It is much easier to find a television program on a prize fight than one on Shakespeare. As the English philosopher, C. E. M. Joad put it, "those things which are peculiar to each of us and may in their forms of expression well be different in all of us, cannot be catered for in bulk by commercial agencies." When a man wishes to enjoy an individual pleasure, even though it be an unadvertised cigarette, or a page of

18

Pepys' Diary, he has to isolate himself from those who cater to the mob.

Most pleasures today are associated with movement, and in the case of the young, with speed. A quick change of scenery and pace seems to be one of the ingredients of modern enjoyment. One out of every four persons in the United States changes his address during the year. The unquiet mind makes an unquiet body. Novelists move more than philosophers or thinkers, because the novelists generally write about sense-experiences while philosophers write about thoughts. Socrates never left Greece, Kant was never outside Koenigsberg, Bach was permanently at Leipzig while Schubert spent most of his life around Vienna. But today many novelists leave their country in search of new experiences. There is some connection between stationariness of the body and the acquisition of the superior truths of the spirit. It is only the quiet pool that reflects the stars.

After a body is surfeited with pleasures, it reaches a point where there is less satisfaction in the pleasure than in the pursuit of it. Not to be someplace, but the thrill of speeding there, becomes the goal of life. Joyce Kilmer in his delightful poem ''Pennies'' pictures a boy holding some pennies in his hand. The pleasure of getting them is all gone and he is bored with their possession. Suddenly he drops his pennies; seeing them scatter and roll about, all his zest for acquiring returns. When the pennies no longer satisfied, he substituted the new pleasure of hunting them. There is not a millionaire who did not say: ''I will retire when I get a million.'' The million bored him, then his pleasure was not in having money, but in pursuing it.

As the human mind loses an objective and a goal in life, even its culture becomes identified with movement as pleasure, instead of the attainment of a goal. Modern writing reflects this inasmuch as it is made up of experiences strung together, but leading nowhere, nor painting any moral. Minds never inquire where they came from, or where they are going; they are just on the way. They never begin, they never develop, they never end—they just stop. Nothing in life has a shape, a pattern, a rule or destiny. Nothing links things together except more succession in time; the needle of writing is drawn through the cloth but it weaves no pattern.

A man cannot talk with his mouth full. His thinking processes are impeded in direct relation to the intensity of the exercise of his sensible satisfactions. The more intense the sensible reaction, the less the concentration of thought. This is the basis for two important truths: first, lust does, as Scripture says, impede the spirit and the mind. The second is that the pleasures of the body do play an important role in aiding the soul. It is this very power of relaxation attached to sensible pleasure which proves such a boon to the man; it rests his soul, and when pleasure does that, it is really pleasurable.

CHAPTER FIVE

Moods

AT ONE TIME it was believed that the sun moved about the earth; indeed, it did seem so to the eye, as we saw it purpling the dawn, and at night "setting like a host in the flaming monstrance of the West." But now we know that the earth moves about the sun.

As there were two ways of looking at the relation of the earth and the sun—one right and one wrong— so there are two ways of looking at the relation between a person and the daily events and routine cycle of life. Some people live in such a way as to have all their moods determined by what happens to them in the world. They are sad when stars take up their encampment on the battlefield of night; and they are gay in morning's eyes. When there is rain on the cheek of nature, often tears bedew their own cheeks. What happens at the bargain counter, in the office or in traffic; the poisoned arrow of sarcasm, the overheard slur and the whining of children, so often make and mold our moods, that like chameleons we take on the color of the experience that presently imposes itself on us. When we allow ourselves to revolve about circumstances, our feelings become like the sea-

sons, shrinking when some hard service must be done
and fainting in the face of every woe. Even love is
reduced to fickleness, so that the only love songs one
hears now on radio and television are about "how
happy we will be" when married; no longer does one
hear the "silver threads among the gold," or the story
of how happy the couple is that said they would be
happy with "a girl for you, a boy for me." As Edna
St. Vincent Millay expressed it:

"I know I am but summer to your heart
And not the full four seasons of the year."

The condition of a happy life is to so live that the
trials and vicissitudes of life do not impose their
moods on us. Rather, we become so rooted in peace
and inner joy that we communicate them not only
to our surroundings, but also to others. Tennyson
spoke of such a character "with power on thine own
act and on the world." Some radiate cheer and happiness because they already have it within them, just
as some seem to have ice on their foreheads, making
winter all the year.

The problem is how to possess this inner constancy of peace which makes the depths of our soul
calm, even when the surface like the ocean, is ruffled
or mixed with storms or cares. The best way is prayer
which gives us independence of moods in two ways:
first, it exhausts our bad moods, by telling them to
God. The wrong way is to exhaust our bad feelings
on human beings, because either they resent them,
plan revenge, or they reciprocate by assuming an
equally bad mood. Bringing them to God is exhaust-
ing them, just like bringing ice to the flame melts the
ice. A very false theory in modern psychology is that
whenever we feel pent up psychologically, we should
give it a physiological outlet—for example, "forget it;
go out and get drunk," or "when the passions are

strong, satisfy them." If every son-in-law did this with a mother-in-law who was "moody" with him, the population of the country would be reduced by one-tenth. It is right to say that the mood must be emptied, but to empty it on ourselves, or on our fellow man, is to get it back either with a hangover or an enslaved condition we cannot break.

The second advantage of prayer is not only to void our bad moods, but to replace them with good feelings. As we pray, the sense of God's presence and law becomes more intimate; instead of wanting to "get even with our enemy," we take on God's attitude toward them, which is loving forgiveness and mercy. We may even reach a point, if we pray enough, where we become unsatisfied until we render good for evil. Gradually we see that it is far sadder to be a wrong-doer than to be the wronged one; the injurer is much more to be pitied than the injured. Eventually we get rid of moods, cultivate a constancy which never retaliates, even as Stephen did, who after the example of Our Lord, forgave those who stoned him. In the strains of life, nothing is as soothing and as strengthening as the comforting power of prayer.

CHAPTER SIX

A Period of Drift

WE ARE LIVING in what might be called a Period of
Drift. The snow piles in drifts according to the varia-
tions of the winds. So, too, in certain moments of
history minds are driven by every wind of doctrine
and theory, lacking all standards by which to judge
and evaluate what is happening to them. Sometimes it
is called Chance; others label it Fate. Whatever it be
named, it is an abandon to outside forces, a passivity
and nonresistance to waves which toss the ship at
their mercy. One finds it in Europe, as people say:
"Why build a home? Another war will come to destroy it." We find it in America in a refusal to ex-
amine the causes of our tribulations.

The great difference between a Christian or moral
civilization and our post-Christian civilization is this:
The former regarded the world as a scaffolding up
through which souls climbed to the Kingdom of
Heaven. When the last soul shall have climbed up
through it, the scaffolding will be torn down and
burned with fervent fire, not because it is base, but
simply because it has done its work—it has brought us
back again to God. This meant that there were always

AVE MARIA SHOP
3650 STEVENS CREEK BLVD
SAN JOSE, CALIF. 95117

2 5 JAN 72

$00.50 —
$00.03 TAX

$00.53 TOTAL

a set of values and a cargo of judgments by which the actions of the political and economic and social world could be judged at any one moment. These measurements were distinct from the world in which we moved, just as the tape measure is apart from the cloth. One knew whether or not he was making progress because there was always a fixed point of arrival.

In our contemporary civilization, there are no fixed points. We keep changing them and calling them progress. It is like playing basketball with a changing target; the point of the game at one moment is shooting the ball through the rim; the next minute it is to hit the referee; the next second it is to hit a movable basket which changes its location like a mechanical rabbit at a dog track. Nobody seems to be sure about the purpose of life, hence many become discouraged about living; any trip loses its zest unless there is a destination.

The Sense of Drift is characterized by the inanity that the meaning of the world lies in the world itself; that the electric bulb has no explanation in an Edison outside the bulb itself; that the poem is explicable by the meter, the painting by the colors. This desire to be lost in the stream of nature without goal or purpose or origin is what made Chesterton remark laconically: "I wish I were a jelly fish that couldn't fall downstairs."

One of the fallacies of being immersed in the current is that we have no standard of judging whether we ought to be there or not. When men take their beliefs entirely from the civilization in which they live, they can never know whether those beliefs are right or wrong. Then there is no difference between a fish in the ocean and a drowning man in the ocean—both are in the current and there is nothing outside the current to determine why one should be there and not the other. Once it is denied that men have no other standards than those taken from the quicksands in which they are living, then they can never be induced to build their houses on rocks.

The way out of this Sense of Drift is for men to disentangle themselves from the world in which they live; to see that there is a world of difference between what they *do* and what they *ought* to do; between their ideals and their behavior; between what is "willed" in their present situation and what is "unwilled." If the world is drifting to war, it is because enough people in the world have a sense of acquiescence to the drift, or because they have been dulled by some opiate which makes them believe that everything that happens resides in circumstances outside the victim's control.

To get out of a snowdrift, a man has to realize that he ought not to be in a snowdrift. To get out of the mess the world is in, man has to realize three things: 1) He was not made for drifting, but for self-perfection and happiness; 2) This happiness can be thwarted freely by consenting to imperfection, to evil and to sin; 3) But even when we consent to evil, there is still a way out and that is by having recourse to the Divine. This is sanctity, not politics.

could beat him at bridge.'' The ''I's'' come very close together, as they do in all intellectual narrowness.

This egotism can be very cleverly disguised, sometimes by boasting of self, sometimes by making oneself appear ridiculous, sometimes by overrating self, other times by underrating oneself. ''I flung off that book in two weeks,'' being interpreted this means: ''Think of what it would have been if I had worked on it fifteen days.'' This egotism eventually reaches a point where it inflicts pain on others through its snobbery. Franz Werfel, in a remarkable autobiographical passage says: *''I have experienced many varieties of arrogance, in myself and in others. But since I myself shared these varieties for a time in my youth, I must confess from personal experience that there is no more consuming, more insolent, more sneering, more diabolical arrogance than that of the artistic advance guard and radical intellectuals, who are bursting with a vain mania to be deep and dark and subtle and to inflict pain. Amid the amused and indignant laughter of hell of a few Philistines, we were the indignant stokers who preheated the hell in which mankind is now roasting.''*

The third stage which is growth into maturity and represents escape from egotism is attained when one mounts from the ''me'' and the ''I'' to the ''Thou'' or the love of neighbor. The ''Thou'' is understood as a person of inviolable worth, bearing within himself the Divine image, the bearer of those ineradicable rights which are the foundation of all democracy, and endowed with aspirations which make him either a real or potential child of God. The neighbor is not necessarily the one close to me. Conceivably he could be next door and be an enemy, and yet he would still be a neighbor. What does ''next door'' mean anyhow? Horizontally or vertically? Horizontally, the neighbor could mean the man who throws his grass over my back fence after he mows his lawn. But vertically, it could mean the man in China, for if I go in a straight line through my land, I may turn up a Chinese or a Tibetan.

The neighbor is the mysterious undistinguishable person who happens to cross my path at any moment, either in a friendly or unfriendly fashion. The neighbor is the one who steps on my toes in the subway, or who makes a left turn from the outside lane in Sunday traffic, or who grabs the dress out of your hands at a bargain counter when you want it, or who talks an hour on the party line when you want to use it, or who sneaks ahead of you the bus for a seat, or who asks to use your home projector and then inflicts homemade movies on you for an evening. The neighbor is not someone you like; he could just as well be someone we do not like and yet one we are under the commandment to love: *"Thou shalt love thy neighbor as thyself."*

Spiritual maturity is reached when we love each "thou" that we meet with something of the same love we bear ourselves; pardoning when they do wrong, praising when they do right, finding excuses in the same way we excuse ourselves. It is not of great moment to be constantly asking ourselves if we love our neighbor. What is important is to act out that love. We learn to walk by walking, to play by playing and to love by loving. If we do anybody whom we hate a good turn, we find that we hate him less; if we do him an evil turn, we discover that we hate him more. Doing kind acts to people makes us find all people lovable. And if love is not there, we put it there and then everyone becomes lovable.

CHAPTER EIGHT

Failure and Success

THE SOULS OF MEN are tried less by work than by
the frustration that comes from too much attention
to the trivial. Most of us live on the surface of the
soul. We make investigations in every direction until
we come to the frame of the picture; but few go outside of it to ask the name of the author. Few are
ready to obey Our Lord's injunction to Peter on the
Sea of Galilee: *"Launch out into the deep and let
down your nets for a draught."* When Peter received
this order, he replied that all attempts at sounding
depths had resulted in failure: *"Master, we have labored all the night and have taken nothing; nevertheless at Thy Word....."*

It may be that we have been endeavoring to make
enough to support a family, to master a trade, to ful-
fill a vocation, to find a job, but nothing seems to
have prospered. The Divine injunction is not to
cease. At His Word lower the net once again. Duty
must always take precedence over pleasure; recreation
is the reward of work not a preparation for it and
therefore must always be earned. Very often God is
prepared to help us most when we admit that of and

by our own power we can do nothing. *"At Thy Word"* becomes the watchword of the moral heroes. By that trust they align themselves with the Power of Him from Whose fingertips tumbled planets and worlds. An ark is built on dry land; a motley crowd gathers round about to pour scorn and ridicule on bearded Noah. Unashamed, he lifted his face to the heavens saying: *"I have built this vessel, O God, at Thy Word."* Not because of success, but in spite of it Peter said: *"But at Thy Word I will let down the net."* Empty nets without His Blessing, but full nets with it. The night of failure was not without the lesson. We can do worse than fail; we can succeed and be proud of our success and burn incense to our nets and despise those who fail and forget the Hand which both gives and withholds.

When Peter obeyed, his net enclosed a great multitude of fishes. Success came after failure, but not after the abandonment of effort. He who would say: *"I slept at my post,"* or *"I refuse to cast any more nets,"* or *"I have allowed weariness to make me lazy, and disappointment to make me hopeless"* can never expect the Lord to supply his deficiencies. Thus the meaning of the oft-quoted truth: *"The Lord helps those who help themselves."* That is, we must work as if everything depended on us and trust as if everything depended on Him. Not infrequently, the work of which we have the least hope in the end gives us the most joy.

The miracle of the great catch of fishes prompted Peter to fall at the feet of Our Lord saying: *"Depart from me, O Lord, for I am a sinful man."* It was a cry of despairing love, not despairing hate; the cry of one who aspires after the infinite and realizes how unworthy he is of its blessings. Man for the most part is unconscious of his *moral* failures; his *physical*

CHAPTER NINE

The Psychology of Man and Woman

EDUCATION TODAY makes no difference between the training of man and woman. This is right from the point of view of opportunities that are open to both; but it is short-sighted when one considers the psychological differences between the two.

The first obvious difference between the two, and the one most often pointed out, is that man is rational and woman intuitive. The man often stands bewildered and confused at what are called a "woman's reasons." They completely escape his understanding, because they cannot be analyzed, taken apart and arranged in an orderly sequence. Her conclusions seem to come as a "whole piece"; there are no vestibules to the house of her arguments; you walk right into the parlor of a conclusion, and it seems, often by a trap door. The very immediacy of her conclusions startles a man because they obtrude without any apparent foundation. But they are just as unshakable as the reasoned deduction of the male.

A second difference is that a man governs the home, but the woman reigns in it. Government is related to justice and law; reigning, to love and feeling. The orders of the father in a home are like written mandates from a king; the influence of the woman, however, is more subtle, more felt and less aggressive. The commands of the father are more jerky and intermittent; the quiet pervading radiation of the mother is constant, like the growth of a plant. And yet both are essential for the home, for justice without love could become tyranny, and love without justice could become toleration of evil.

A third difference is how they react as on one hand to trifles, such as the souring of cream and, on the other hand the great crises, such as the loss of a job. Man is much less disturbed by trifles, with the exception of the morning paper being taken by the neighbor's dog. The daily shocks of life disturb man less; the little things are like drops of water he can absorb in the sponge of his masculinity. The woman, however, is more readily upset by inconsequential things, possessed as she is by a rare talent of turning molehills into mountains.

But when it comes to the great crises of life, it is the woman, in virtue of her gentle powers of reigning who can give great consolation to man in his troubles. She can recover reason and good sense, at the very moment the man seems to lose his. When the husband is remorseful, sad and disquieted, she brings comfort and assurance. As the ocean is ruffled on the surface but calm in the depths, so in a home, the man is the rippled surface, the woman the deep and quiet stability.

A fourth difference is that woman is less satisfied with mediocrity than man. This may be because man is more attached to the material and the mechanical, and woman more to the biological and the living. The closer one gets to the material, the more one becomes materialized. Nothing so dulls the soul for the finer values of life as counting. But the woman, being the bearer of life, is less indifferent to great values, more quickly disillusioned with the material and the human. This may account for the judgment often made that religion is more natural for women than for men. This is not because woman is more timid and is more likely to seek flight and refuge in the spiritual; it is rather because being less trapped by the material, she is more likely to pursue ideals that transcend the earthly.

These differences, instead of being opposites, are actually in a marriage correlated. Man is like the roots of a plant; woman more like the blossom that bears the fruit. One is in communion with the earth and business; the other with the sky and life. One is related to time; the other to eternity. The fusion of both is the prolongation into the home of the Incarnation where Eternity became time and the Word became flesh, and the Divine became the human in the person of Christ. Differences are not irreconcilable; rather they are complementary qualities. The functional differences correspond with certain psychic differences, which make one in relation to the others like the violin and the bow, producing the music of a home and the joys of a marriage that symbolize the mystical marriage of Christ and His Bride, the Church.

CHAPTER TEN

There's Good in the Bad

WHEN WE FIND imperfections in people we generally stop loving them. This may be the very reason they remain imperfect, because they have no one to love them into perfection. There are many amiable qualities in the unregenerate; even in a decayed condition there are remnants of honesty and decency. One great sin in a person sometimes by its nature excludes other sins; therefore there is something in them to love. The spendthrift, for example, is never covetous; the Communists with their passion for power and revolution often put lust far down in the scale of human enjoyments. As certain weeds destroy other weeds, so do many vices; the prodigal son was probably a very likeable individual from the social point of view.

One day a rich young ruler came to Our Divine Lord. He asked what he must do to attain everlasting life. Our Lord told him to keep the commandments. The young man said that he had done that from his youth. Our Lord then told him if he would be perfect: "Go, sell all thou hast, give to the poor, then come, follow Me." The young man, we are told, went away sad, because he had great possessions, which he was unwilling to surrender. But the Gospel says: "Our Lord loved him" despite his obvious imperfections. What sticks in the minds of most of us in that story is the fact that the young man refused to be a spiritual hero. But Our Saviour knew that the young man could never be a spiritual hero unless he was loved in his unspiritual weakness.

Once we allow the distasteful aspects of a character to fade away, and no longer concentrate on them, the good qualities begin immediately to appear. This often happens when a person dies; while alive his bad points seemed like blots on a scutcheon, but after death there begin to appear good qualities which we had never suspected. Our Divine Lord takes the same view of men while they are alive that we often take after their demise.

Very likely the Divine insight saw that every bad quality is a perversion of a good quality. Insincerity could be due to a refusal to hurt other people's feelings; lavishness could be the reverse side of an instinct toward generosity; love of luxury could be the upside down of a love of perfection, except that instead of luxuriating the soul in virtue, the body is enriched. Abruptness is the reverse of a desire to be straightforward; a critical spirit might well be the dark side of the will to be just and righteous, but for the moment instead of reforming self one starts out to reform everybody else.

In the case of the young man, the fact that he was rich was of little moment; what was important was that he trusted in his riches more than anything else. It was the summons of the Redeemer that brought out that weakness. There are some people who trust God when they have a big bank account. This young man had many fine qualities; he wanted to inherit

eternal life; he had kept all the commandments from
his youth; he had humility enough to confess his
desire for moral betterment on a public highway in
the face of curious passers-by. What he lacked was total
and complete allegiance; the spirit of the soldier who
asks only what are his marching orders.

Hence the Master told him he "lacked but one
thing." No one is very far from perfection and inner
peace. As Leon Bloy once said: "One step beyond
mediocrity and we are saved." A watch with jewels
without a mainspring; the sun dial without its iron
finger; the ship without the rudder—all these lack but
one thing. Multiply zeros; they lack one thing. Put a
1 or a 2 in front of them and they become great
sums. One habitual fault can vitiate a whole life.
But even when that one thing is lacking, if we do not
love a sun dial enough to give it the iron finger, or
if we do not love the ship enough to give it the
rudder, they will forever be useless. So it is with
characters; unless we love them we will never supply
the one thing needful for their reformation, their
happiness and their inner peace.

HABITS

CHAPTER ELEVEN

Habits

CONFUCIUS WROTE: "The nature of man is always the same; it is their habits that separate them." The Spanish have a proverb which elaborates this into: "Habits are at first cobwebs, then cables." Habits are specifically human and deserve more consideration than is generally given to them. Animals, for example, never develop habits in the strict sense of the term, because their growth in perfection is fixed within definite biological limits. It is true that a dog may bring in the morning paper, but this is only because he has been trained to act that way by his master's reason. Left to himself, the dog would tear up the paper at six months, bark at the delivery boy at nine months, run around in circles when told to pick it up at fourteen months, and at three years ignore it completely.

Because we are capable of developing habits in different directions, it follows that habits can be good or bad, according to their purpose or the goal toward which they are directed. A skill can be developed in handling a knife: a surgeon may cut a neck to remove a goiter or a gangster may cut a throat to remove a rival. Every habit either helps a man attain his eternal end, which is God, or else it impedes and confuses by forging a chain which is difficult to break. Hamlet tried to get his mother to give up illicit relations with the plea:

"Refrain tonight,
And that shall lend a kind of easiness
To the next abstinence; the next more easy;
For use almost can change the stamp of nature."

The great advantage of habit is that it saves us a lot of attention, effort and brain work. Driving an automobile would be as nerve racking as when we first learned it, if nature did not make it automatic. Thanks to habit there is now a conservation and strengthening of what is good. Too often the word "habit" is used in relation to what is evil, e.g., the "drinking habit," the "stealing habit," the "swearing habit." But habit can refer to what is good such as the "habit of prayer," the "habit of charity," the "habit of self-denial." In this case, habit is called "virtue." Our receptive and expansive nature stands ready to incorporate such pieties into the fibre of its spontaneous movements. Virtue then becomes as easy to one person as vice to another.

As C. K. Walpole has written: "Could the young realize how soon they will become walking bundles of habits, they would give more heed to their conduct in their plastic state. Every smallest stroke of virtue or vice leaves its ever so little scar. The drunken *Rip Van Winkle,* in Jefferson's play, excuses himself for every fresh dereliction by saying: 'I won't count this time.' He may not count it, and a kind Heaven may not count it, but it is being counted none the less. Down among the nerve cells and fibres, the molecules are counting it, registering it, and storing it up to be used against him when the next temptation comes. Nothing we ever do is, in strict scientific literalness, wiped out. As we become permanent drunkards by so many separate drinks, so we become saints in the moral, authorities and experts in the practical and scientific spheres, by so many separate acts and hours of work.''

Educators and parents will realize that the habits which make a man wise do not necessarily make a man good. Intellectual habits will make a man a good violinist but will not make him moral. Education today concentrates on mental habits or knowledge, but not on moral habits or character. The secret roots of modern anxiety, fear and tension are not hidden in pre-natal influences as Freud was so fond of saying; they are hidden in patterns of behavior which eventually enslaved the victim. He who will not follow virtue or good habits in youth cannot escape neuroses in old age. But he who has virtue cannot only sustain bad fortune; he is not swept off his feet even by good fortune.

CHAPTER TWELVE

Need of a Vacation

REST never seems to be where we are, but otherwhere. Then when we get there, it seems to have gone somewhere else. Al Smith once said: "The two best days of vacation are the day you leave home, and the day you get back." Rest is the imperative of creation. Even the earth that whirls on its axis has its stated seasons of light and darkness. The farmer knows that the soil is more productive when there is a rotation of crops, or when a field is allowed every now and then to lie fallow. Outdoor workers have the law of repose most clearly impressed on their minds, for "the night cometh when no man can work." What Nature imposes by law, man is supposed to know by reason. "God in creating nature labored for six days and then rested," thus giving man the pattern of life. The many flowers that fell from His creative Hands that closed their petals at night, and the birds which cover their heads with their wings are so many poetical and rhythmic whispers to man that he too must seek his repose.

Psychology confirms Nature in this law which the Saviour expressed to His Apostles after many days of hard labor. "Come ye apart and rest awhile." The brain has certain areas wherein certain functions are localized, such as seeing, hearing, etc. When one area functions for a long time to the exclusion of other functions, and without any intermission, mental depression and fatigue set in. It is very much like using one set of muscles alone in the human body; the want of proportionate use of all then induces extra fatigue and tension. A baseball pitcher who throws only with his arm, without putting his whole body behind the motion, rarely lasts nine full innings, or an entire season.

Even the development of the mind along one line alone, without cultivating universal interests, is apt to beget a narrowness of vision and even an intolerance.

There is nothing which so much dulls the human spirit as counting; unless the addiction to the enumeration of materialities is compensated for by more spiritual interests, the mind loses its capacities not only for abstract thinking, but also for a humane outlook on life. Darwin said at the close of his life that he regretted he had completely lost all taste for music and poetry as a result of concentration on plants and animals. The lower sciences which deal only with materialities often penalize the specialists with an exclusiveness which amounts almost to blindness. Unless there is a development of the brain and the mind with other interests than those of experimentation, one can falsely lead himself into believing that there is nothing in the world except what he touches and sees.

The demand for rest is almost psychologically imposed on those who do physical work, like pitching hay, digging ditches, stringing telephone wires and shucking corn. But the mental workers are more apt to be caught in the whirl and think their business and their duties are so important that they cannot take a day off from their work. This is apt to be the great fault of the American businessman who works until he can never take a rest; he gets so involved in the building of more barns that he has gotten hold of an electric wire which he cannot let go. The wear and tear of mental work in offices and in business is probably far more taxing on the system than any physical work. And yet such "busy people" talk, think and do business so incessantly that the only time off they take is ten minutes to watch a steam shovel prepare to dig a foundation for another sky-scraper. Even then, it is dubious if they relax, for building contractors now drill holes in fences around construction projects with the inscription: "Sidewalk inspectors," thus indicating that at least mentally they are still in the business mood.

Henry Ward Beecher once said that he could do a year's work in eleven months, but he could not do it in twelve. He knew that the bow that is always bent loses its strength.

CHAPTER THIRTEEN

Architecture and Courtesy

MODERN ARCHITECTURE is without decoration; modern life is without courtesy. Is there any connection between the two? When buildings appear without ornamentation, do human relations begin to lack good manners? Let us see.

Architecture is a reflection of a philosophy of life. The basic philosophy of the contemporary world is materialism, or the denial of the spirit. But if there is no world above that which can be seen, touched and scientifically analyzed, then there never can be ornamentation, for ornamentation is symbolism or the communication of the non-material through the material. Ornamentation implies another world beyond this. The U.N. Building and the new buildings which appear on Park Avenue in New York, resemble illuminated cracker boxes, or elongated shoe boxes on stilts. They are purely "functional" because the only function of a material civilization is business and the exchange of things of this world.

When civilization was permeated with a more happy philosophy; when the things that were seen were regarded as signs and outward expressions of

the things that were not seen, architecture was en-
hanced with a thousand decorations: a pelican feed-
ing her young from her own veins symbolized the
sacrifice of Christ; the lion breathing new life into
her dead cubs represented the Resurrection; the fox
peeking his head around the corner was a warning
against the wiles of Satan. Our Lord on the occasion
of His triumphant entrance into Jerusalem said that
if men held their praise of Him, the very "stones
would cry out"—which they did indeed in Gothic
Cathedrals. Now the stones are silent, for modern
man believes there is no other world, no other destiny than that of the stone itself.

When faith in the spiritual is lost, architecture has
nothing to express or symbolize. In like manner, when
men lose the conviction that everyone is endowed
with an immortal soul and, therefore, is worth more
than the universe, there is naturally a decline in respect for the human. Man without a soul is a thing,
and a thing is something to be used, not something
to be reverenced. He becomes "functional" like a
building or a monkey wrench or a wheel. The
courtesies, amenities, urbanity and gentility that one
mortal ought to have for another are lost, once man
is no longer seen as bearing within himself the Divine
Image.

The supreme dignity of the human person, which is
the foundation of democracy, is also the foundation
of courtesy; but when a man is a tool, not a little
less than the angels, human relations then become as
devoid of courtesy as the U.N. Building of ornamentation: what decoration is to a building, courtesy is
to life—a sign and symbol that there is more than is
seen, and that behind every interchange of human
relations is imperceptibly woven a love that is the
reflection of Love Divine. The name of a friend pro-

nounced with reverence and affection is like a stone in a Cathedral crying out the glory of God. Gentleness and refinement can thrive only where there is a sense of the sacredness of personality. Even the word "kind" comes from the old English word "kin." The kind person was a "kinned" person, one who shared the same blood and enjoyed the same fruits of redemption. Hence mankind was originally "menkinned"—all related as brothers because God was the common Father.

Courtesy is not a condescension of a superior to an inferior, or a patronizing interest in another's affairs. It is the homage of the heart to the sacredness of human worth. It brings graciousness into conversation, as the tone of the voice, the gesture of the body, the response of the eye and the little grace notes of action, reveal that we are addressing someone with an immortal destiny and one for whom Christ died. Courtesy is born of holiness as ornamentation is born of the sense of Holy. Let us just watch and see if, when ornamentation returns to architecture, that courtesy also returns to manners.

WILL

CHAPTER FOURTEEN

The Right Drive for Superiority

THE MOST COMMON JUDGMENT passed today on others is: "Oh, he has an inferiority complex." It would be much truer to say of those really so complicated that they have a superiority complex, that is an unjustified drive toward superiority. But even here, it is well to remember that there is a right and wrong kind of superiority. The wrong kind of superiority is domination over others, pride, boastfulness, egotism, self-will and cruelty. The right kind of superiority is striving for self-protection in the moral order.

Our Blessed Lord suggested that we be satisfied with nothing less than perfection: "Be ye perfect as your Heavenly Father is perfect." This does not mean that we are to be perfect as God is perfect, but to be perfect in a God-like and not a human way.

What is startling about this command is that we are bidden not to imitate others, but God. The Divine Master would produce not character, but a better character. To Him, it is not great virtue to love those who love us. If such be the case, He asks: "What title have you to reward? Will not the publicans do as much?" Virtue to Him was not democratic, but aristocratic; it was high above the mass-level, not one that struck the happy medium between the good and the bad. The crux of virtue is not on the number of those who practice it, but in its principles. "Everybody is doing it" may determine democratic practices, but it is not character or virtue.

"What are you doing more than others?"—that is the acid test. He who thinks he has done enough, has done nothing. The regularities of constitutional goodness, the observance of common decencies, politeness, generosity, good cheer, the good affections which nature prompts—these are the perfection of the common man, not of God. There are few men who would not claim to some moral distinction if they were honest, and paid their income taxes, gave to the poor, and allowed other men their point of view. But it appears that even when we have done these excellencies, we may still be asked by the standard of Divine Superiority: "What are you doing more than others?"

It is common today to identify a Christian with a gentleman, or a "nice chap." Certainly we should strive to have a world in which there are as many nice people as possible, such as those who give their seats to ladies in subways, who speak with appreciation of the United Nations, who help old women across the street and are kind to the deaf. But we must not make the mistake of believing that by that fact they have become Christian. As a Professor of Philosophy at Cambridge said recently in a television address: "A world of nice people, content in their own goodness, niceness, looking no further, turned away from God, would be just as much in need of salvation as a miserable world—and might even be more difficult to save."

The superiority for which men strive today is generally economic or social, not spiritual or moral. When one hears of those who leave the mass-level and dedicate themselves to spiritual perfection, the tendency is to argue: (1) There is nothing in it but an "escape." (2) Those who pretend to see something in it are posing. (3) I hate them for it. The reason there is a hatred is because these people in the end may be having something that I do not have.

No personality is adequately expressed on the average level. The common man from a moral point of view is common. He who tries to keep on the level with others has already condemned himself to failure. The development of spiritual personality is in going the extra mile and challenging the conventional morality. "If someone compels thee to attend him on a mile's journey," said Our Lord, "go two miles with him of thy own accord." The weakness of our age is in want of great men. It is hard for men to resist the current. Someone must completely detach himself from the ordinary run of politicians, if he is to save politics; economists must break with the ordinary run of the mill of capital and labor commonplaces, if economics is to be saved. In other words, we need saints. These are not easy to make. First of all—because man does not always want the best; the best demands sacrifice of the ordinary and the discipline of the lower self. God, in His turn, finds it hard to

CHAPTER FIFTEEN

Good on the Inside

IF GOODNESS on the outside is not the release of goodness on the inside, it is show or hypocrisy. What the rudder is to the ship, what the spring is to the watch, that the heart is to actions. It is the mint where evil deeds and good deeds are coined; the anvil on which is forged behavior; the blueprint of the edifice of life. As the pulse beat is healthy or ill according to the condition of the heart, so a man in his life is what he is already in his thoughts and desires.

Nothing shows more thoughtlessness than the idiocy that "it makes no difference what you believe; it all depends on the way you live." On the contrary, we act on our beliefs; our ideas are motorsprings in action; if our thinking is bad our actions will be bad. Would we say it made no difference to the editor of a newspaper if each of his readers believed that he should be shot? Let everybody believe that way and the editor soon will be shot.

Many men are perverted from carrying out their beliefs in action; that is why there are insane asylums. A vicious horse is not the more gentle animal when

he is bound with kicking straps. Our Divine Lord
said that even though our evil thoughts could not
be actualized, the evil act was nevertheless to be im-
puted to us as guilt. "Any man looking after a woman
and lusting after her has already committed adultery
with her in his own heart." If it is wrong to do a
certain thing, it is wrong to think about that thing.
If it is wrong to stuff Aunt Sophie's mattress with
old razor blades, it is wrong to think about doing it.
Keep the thoughts clean and the behavior will be
good.

Environment may condition our lives, but it does
not determine them. Adam lived in a good environment but produced an act of rebellion. Judas lived
in an excellent environment but he betrayed his
Saviour; many Americans live in the environment of
the most prosperous country in the world, but they
sell out to the tyranny of slavery. With justice then
did Our Divine Saviour say: "Nothing that goeth
into a man from without can defile him; but the
things that come out of him are what defile a man."

Environment, economic conditions and grand-
mothers who love too much or too little are circumstances that do help to make a man, but they make
him only to the degree he permits them to make
him. Our American life would be healthier if our
politics and our education more generally struck the
same note. Our politics insist on freedom: freedom of
press, suffrage, choice of work, etc. But much education teaches that man is not responsible; either his
glands, or his want of playgrounds, or the lack of
dance halls made him what he is; therefore he is not
responsible for what he does. But to say he is not
responsible is to say that he is not free. Our political concepts are right; these particular educational
theories are wrong.

If we are free we are self-determining; if we are self-determining then our actions are *willed* from the inside; if they are willed from the inside then "Blessed are the clean of heart, for they shall see God."

CHAPTER SIXTEEN

Wanting to Be Good

THERE IS ONLY ONE REASON why we are not better, and that is because we do not *will* to be better. We *want* to be better, but wanting is wishing. Willing is decision implemented by action. Most of us make the same reservations about our moral betterment that we do about dieting: "We will start tomorrow." As St. Augustine said "I want to be chaste, dear Lord, but a little later on." The thinnest border line between opposites is in the realm of the spirit. There is an abyss between poverty and wealth, a line that few can cross unless external circumstances and good fortune are present. The dividing line between ignorance and learning is also wide, for with the best of intentions both leisure and talents which are beyond personal power are necessary. But the line between sin and virtue, between mediocrity and sanctity is the thinnest of all, for all that is required is an efficacious act of our will in cooperation with God's grace. As Leon Bloy put it: "One step beyond mediocrity and we are saved."

Our will is full of excuses, which are half-conscious because we refuse to face them. The more we rebel

against examining our reservations, the more certain
it is that these are the very ones that must be given
up. We are like ships with our sails full of good intentions but we make no progress because we are an-
chored to the depths. The key to the spiritual ad-
vancement is to be found in the Creed: "He de-
scended into hell; the third day He rose again." The
individual must make a descent into his subcon-
sciousness, into his "reservation," the assumptions of
his life, which he does not see, but which he sees
through. Every mind has windows. Through them we
look at reality. We see reality, but we forget that our
windows are colored, and therefore reality is dis-
colored or even disfigured. Prejudice, habits of sin,
avarice, jealousy, each of these gives a different tint
to life's great objectives. If one does not have God
as the Supreme love of life, he has a tin god, or what
psychologists call an ego-ideal by which he judges
everything he sees and hears. He who thinks life consists in titillation of nerve endings of the body
becomes utterly incapable of judging the joys of the
spirit. Everything in this state seems easy and
pleasant to us which flatters the ego-image, but
everything is hard or foolish which is related to God.
The coward who is afraid to face sacrifice of his
lower motivations covers up his want of love by hate,
as Richard III tried to cover up his weakness by
violence: "I am determined to prove a villain." Just
as sometimes our dreams are our disguised wishes, so
too these reservations destroy our conscious attitudes
toward life. Before we can rise from the dead, we
must first go down into the hell of these unconscious
assumptions by a thorough-going self-analysis in the
light of how we stand in God's light. Because egotism
and self-deceit are inseparable, because the more
selfish a person is the more he disguises his deceit, a

ruthless pruning, a pitiless examination of every sub-conscious nook and corner of our minds is necessary to bring out the self as it really is, as distinguished from the ego as it thinks it is. The uprooting of reservations is the essential condition of seeing the Truth. Precisely because Truth is the enemy of deceit, the ego shrinks from facing it. Like Pilate, it turns its back on it and sneers: "What is Truth?"

Nothing so much cripples the spiritual life as these hidden "bugs" in the motor of our soul, such as self-seeking immorality, dishonesty and bitterness toward others. We wonder why, when we seem to advance so far, that we suffer such defeats. Invariably it is because of the "Fifth Column" of prejudices and evil habits and the Trojan horse of dominant fault. Until that is dug out and laid before God, there can be no real progress in the spirit. As St. Augustine said: "He is Thy best servant, O Lord, who looks not so much to hear from Thee what he wants to hear, but rather wills to do that which he hears."

Most of us are a trouble to others, but few want to be a trouble to themselves. They know that a dog cannot be housebroken without trouble and effort, but they expect to make themselves morally good without any effort or self-discipline. Almost all theories of education today leave out self-discipline by which a man pulls and tightens the strings on the violin of his heart until they give forth true melodies. Very few have a plan of action which is broad enough to take in this troubling of the self for the sake of moral perfection. But willing to be better alone is not enough. This decision is merely like opening the blinds; immediately the light floods the darkened spaces. So with the heart: when it admits its need, the grace of God begins to pour into the soul, and out of this conjunction of our will and Divine Power there comes a goodness which is not of this world, and also an inner peace which nothing in this world can destroy.

CHAPTER SEVENTEEN

How Things Go Wrong

IT IS EASY to understand why an alcoholic gets drunk, a robber steals again and an unhappy man criticizes others. But why is it that an habitually sober man may get drunk, a kind person be cruel to another, and an otherwise devoted husband be unfaithful to his wife?

To answer these questions one must make a study of the ideals and the objects which move the will to action. There are two kinds of stimuli or excitants to action—one is called adequate, the other inadequate. In the sensible order, the adequate stimulus of sight is color; the inadequate stimulus may be a red barn; the adequate stimulus of hearing is sound; the inadequate may be a policeman's whistle; the adequate stimulus of curiosity is a strange object which excites wonder; an inadequate object may be a mink coat over baggy slacks. Such improper objects delight or arouse us for the moment, but do not bring complete satisfaction or happiness.

Every faculty or talent we have has some object which is its complete realization, for example, the perfection or adequate object of the mind is truth;

the perfection or adequate object of the will is goodness. One single truth, such as the knowledge of the electrical charges inside an atom, does not completely satisfy the mind, because the mind is made to know the full orbit of truth, not a segment of it. A good meal satisfies the stomach, but a good deed does not exhaust the possibilities of the will; it remains incomplete until the highest and best of its ideals are fulfilled.

If the human mind were suddenly presented with the fullness of truth, that is to say, with Divine Truth which contains within itself all that is knowable and can be known, it would not be free to reject it, because it is for that that the mind was made and which alone can satisfy it. It is like a man finding the ideal woman whom he wants to be his wife. No other can satisfy once the ideal has been discovered. If the will were brought face to face with Divine Love, and saw it dying in a human nature for others, it would be irresistibly drawn to it. In heaven, there will be no more freedom of choice, because once in possession of the perfect, there will be nothing left to desire. And yet, one will still be perfectly free because he has become one with Love and Power that can do all things.

On this earth, we are not confronted with this total object of our existence, which is God; we are pulled hither and thither by imperfect objects, false ideals and tin gods. Nothing that we see or hear or know is so compelling as to be a magnet and pull us toward that which is the perfection of our personality.

Now we are in a position to answer the question posed above. Man being free in his choices, may often substitute an inadequate for an adequate idea; he may deliberately drive off the road though he has the road map before him; he may hit a sour note though the score of music is in front of his eyes. Hot objects are normally required to stimulate heat spots on the skin, but these may sometimes be stimulated by a cold bar of iron on a cold day so that we get the impression of "heat." As skin sometimes mistakes cold for hot, particularly when the eyes are closed, so too a person who blacks out his reason and faith for the moment may substitute a false good for a true good. The drug addict and the Communist, on the contrary, have deliberately determined to pursue an ideal which does not lead to perfect happiness; their ideals are always wrong. It is like deliberately choosing half a babe to the whole babe. The only way they can be deterred is by placing before them adequate ideals which satisfy the whole personality and not a part of it. In the case of the otherwise sober man who gets drunk, there is here only momentary substitution of a false ideal. Generally, the unhappiness that he feels is enough to bring him back again to his senses and the pursuit of the highest ideals. If people only knew it, the emptiness and the void they feel after subscribing to false ideals is really the voice of God saying, "You are on the wrong road. Come back! I am the Way, the Truth and the Life."

The Romantic ideal stressed feelings and emotions; it made an emotional or sentimental outlook on mankind the test of human goodness. Jean Jacques Rousseau, who fostered this ideal, once boasted: ''I believe that there is not in the entire world a more humble man than I.'' Feeling good was made equivalent to being good, provided that one did not regard any one experience or moment in life as the totality of life itself.

The Communist ideal of character is quite different from the foregoing. Here the person is judged, not by himself, but by his relation to the revolutionary class. The good character is he who completely submerges his reason and his will to the reason and the will of the Revolutionary Party. Any deviation from that line spoils character even though in one's heart one knows it is wrong.

There is finally the Christian ideal, which is completely different. It differs from the Communist inasmuch as it puts the value on the *person* rather than the *class;* it departs from the Renaissance ideal because the latter takes account of only this world while the Christian affirms man has infinite aspirations which quite transcend this cosmos of space and time. The Christian finds the Romantic ideal incomplete because it pays little or no attention to the intellect and the will, which are the two faculties which make man different from the feeling animal.

But what is most interesting is how the Christian ideal surpasses the Greek. First of all, the Greek puts emphasis on moderation; the Christian on immoderation. Our Divine Lord said that if anyone forces us to walk one mile with him, we ought to walk another; that we were to forgive our enemies not seven times, but seventy times seven, which in the mathematics of heaven means infinity. More important still, the ideal of Christian character is entirely *outside* human nature. The ideal is to be Christ Himself: "I have given you an example." The pattern is thus not man-made, but God-made. Man makes his standards too often to suit the way he lives. Our Lord told us to make our lives fit the way He lived and died. He gave His life to pay the moral debts of others. "Greater love than this no man hath that a man lay down his life for his friends." Now if He, the Pattern-Man did that, then we who have the same ideal must show equal immoderation in caring for our neighbor's needs. There will be unmeasured generosity which never counts the cost; one will never so much think of a duty that he has to others as much as the love he must bear others. Giving is determined less by one's own choice than it is by the love that one has for the neighbor and his needs.

This ethic of love produces in characters a double effect: greater leniency to the wrongdoer and greater *severity to self*. Greater leniency because one discovers that the condition of his own forgiveness is to forgive others—this makes him more kindly to the sinner. But at the same time he knows that he can never conform to his lofty Ideal unless he takes a chisel into his hand and cuts off huge chunks of egotism and selfishness, pride and avarice from the marble of his nature.

We might just as well face it: the Christian ideal of character demands much more than most of us are willing to do, and those who try to do it still believe they fall short of loving others as they should. Instead of changing that ideal and calling it progress, it might be well to change ourselves and call it character development.

CHAPTER NINETEEN

Where Character Is Made

HARDLY ANYONE today challenges the view that character is made by outside or external influences, such as his home background, his schooling, his poverty or wealth, the propaganda to which he was subjected and the neighborhood in which he was raised. This view could lead to the destruction of responsibility if carried to extremes; and responsibility, it must not be forgotten, is the mark of freedom. Environmental influences only condition, but they do not cause character. Our Lord put His Finger on the cause when He said: "For it is from within, from the hearts of men, that their wicked designs come, their sins of adultery, fornication, murder, theft, covetousness, malice, deceit, lasciviousness, envy, blasphemy, pride and folly. All these evils come from within, and it is these which make a man unclean."

Modern psychology emphasizes the importance of the subconscious, but the Divine Master stresses rather the conscious factor of the intellect and will, that is our knowledge and our decisions. The combination of these two is sometimes called the heart, and from them comes our character, as from the tree comes its fruits.

The heart is the mint wherein the coinage of human life is stamped; it is the anvil which forges habits and routines; it is the "stick" which pilots the plane of life. Sir Walter Scott once said to his son-in-law Lockhart: "We shall never learn to feel and respect our own calling and destiny, until we have taught ourselves to consider everything as moonshine, compared with the education of the heart."

The reform of outward conduct and environment is essential, and it is to this that much civil law is ordained. But it really only deals with the effects and not with the causes; social reformation is only superficial; it is like cutting off the tops of the weeds while the roots are left in the ground. Much social reform attempts to cure problems such as crime and juvenile delinquency by changing environment, such as building more dance halls and swimming pools. One of the difficulties social reform must always face is that it hardly ever goes into operation until things have gotten very bad. As long as the people are not aroused to abuses or evil, they will not support social legislation. It must be remembered that all crimes against society are founded on false and wicked ideas, and until these are altered, society will not be altered. A lion is not gentle once it is behind a cage; a wild horse is not less ill-tempered because of a bridle and kicking stirrups.

Only in a limited sense is it true that circumstances make a man; they make a man only to the extent that a man permits circumstances to make him. It is not so much the outward that influences the inward, as the inward that influences the outward. If the reservoir is to be kept clean, all the streams that pour into it must be pure. Evil has its roots in the heart. "As a man thinks in his heart, so is he." The stalactite pillars to be found in caves give a perfect example of how habits are formed by thoughts. Water on the surface of the earth sinks through the soil and rocks, carrying with it a tiny sediment. These drops fall from the ceiling of the cave to the floor, but as they fall they form an icicle, and little by little the deposit grows into a stone pillar. In like manner, if the thoughts and desires and wishes of the heart carry with them a deposit of our decisions and our thoughts, and if these are evil it will not be long until they build strong pillars of evil habits on the outside; the opposite is true when the thoughts are good, holy and pure.

It is the things that we like that make our character; life is stained only because the heart is impure. Thoughts are the eggs of words, and when the will gives motive power to evil thoughts, they become actual transgressions. No man would be believed who, holding a bucket of muddy water in his hand, said that he drew it from a spring that was crystal clear. The heart is the center of life, the throne where manhood sits and rules; the subconscious holds the thoughts and the desires that have been discarded or else the reflections and desires of the heart that have passed into action. Evil is not a robber that breaks into our house; it is a tenant to whom the house has been rented. But, on the contrary, if we keep our hearts clean and God-like on the inside, we will change our environment.

CHAPTER TWENTY

"Holy Terrors"

"CHILDREN ARE TERRIBLE" is the description often given today of the modern generation. A few decades ago, the expression was: Children are "holy terrors." This is a more adequate expression of the fact, for certainly children are "terrible"—terrible like dogs, that have to be housebroken; colts that have to be tamed to the harness or the saddle; gardens that have to be weeded; potatoes that have to be peeled; bread dough that has to be baked; minds that have to be taught, and traffic lights that have to be obeyed. They are "terrible" in the sense that much attention and love, and even discipline, have to be given them before they begin to yield the fruit still hidden in their beautiful but shaky blossoms.

But, at the same time, they are "holy" terrors in the sense that each has an immortal soul, bears the imprint of the Divine Original; because each one is so precious as to be worthy of redemption, and because each has an angel of God to watch it and these angels always see the Face of the Father in heaven.

Life itself is full of "holy terrors"—fire is a holy terror—a terror when it burns the house; holy when it is made to enkindle the hearth and warm the house. Flesh is a terror when it scorches life; holy when it solders and unifies it. Wine is a terror when touched by undisciplined lips, holy when taken for cheer and companionship. Every responsibility in life is a holy terror, whether it be the gift of song, an oil well, a political appointment or a heart in love.

Why then expect children to be anything else than "holy terrors"? That is the way God meant them to be. Gold in the mine is a holy terror—it has to be purged with fire; wood in the forest is a holy terror; it has to be cut and chiseled; the violin string is a holy terror, it has to be tightened before it gives a melody. Children are like that, and for the parents to excuse themselves on the ground that they need so much time and attention is to forget that in life nothing reaches a state of perfection except through sweat and effort and self-negation.

A sick child is brought to a doctor. The mother is told after the examination: "Make the child take this medicine three times a day for two weeks; it is a little bitter, but it will certainly cure him." A month later the child is still ill. The doctor inquires about the medicine and is told by the mother: "Johnnie would not touch it; it was a little bitter." The mother here only remembered her child was a terror, not that he was holy.

The crime with the primal eldest curse upon it brought forth the question: "Cain, where is thy brother Abel?" In like manner, "Parents, what have you done with your children? Do you reproach yourself for what you have done with your children? Do you reproach yourself for what you have left undone? Have you bowed to every whim, given way to every impulse, surrendered to every tear, forgetful that once the holy is divorced from the terror, then terror becomes terrible, just like weeds take over a garden?"

Sometimes too much is expected of children because it is thought that they will become perfect blocks of marble and images of a man, without a chisel ever knocking off huge blocks of egotism. The child may be thoughtless, but the parents must not be; the child may be selfish, but the parents must be selfless. It is these "holy terrors" which make both our great men and our delinquents and criminals. The latter are terrors because the parents forgot the holy.

CHAPTER TWENTY-ONE

Restoring Stolen Goods

THE MOST INTERESTING tax collector in the history of the world was Zaccheus—if you can call any tax collector "interesting." Physically, he was so short that whenever there was a parade, he always had to climb a tree in order to see it. His name meant "pure," but he was anything but that, for he was a "twenty-five per center," always taking that much at least out of what he collected for his "cut." But the end of the story reveals that he was much better than his neighbors believed him to be.

This particular day Our Blessed Lord came to the village, and Zaccheus, as was his wont, climbed a sycamore tree. People that want for size must make up for it by sagacity. Not many tax collectors in our days, particularly those who are "rich," as was Zaccheus, would humble themselves by elevating themselves in a tree. But Zaccheus was rewarded, for Our Lord saw him and He asked him to take Him home. Whenever the Lord wants to give a favor, He often asks for one.

When the door was closed behind the two of them, the mob outside was angry, not with the tax collec-

tor because he was dishonest, but they were angry
with Our Divine Lord because He ate with disreputable people and sinners. The Saviour's way of looking
at it was that He had found one sheep that went
astray. After a few minutes the conscience of the tax
collector was aroused—for consciences only sleep, they
never die. Zaccheus promised to make amends for
his dishonesty by giving half of his goods to the poor
and restoring fourfold to anyone whom he had
cheated.

Restitution is a duty which a civilization which
stresses profits and money can readily forget. When
anyone has been cheated, when capitalists underpay
their workers, when labor leaders during a strike pour
gasoline into milk destined for hospitals, when radio
and television repair men pile up needless expenses
by a seeming substitution of one tube for another,
when an honest day's work is not given for an honest day's pay, there is no distribution of that
equilibrium and balance of justice which makes the
world livable. Remorse is not enough; shame is not
enough; the balming of dishonesty by saying one
has an Oedipus complex or that one feared his grandmother are not enough; there must be a restoring
of the property that was stolen. If the person who
was cheated cannot be found, there must be a dona-
tion of an equal amount to the poor. Restitution is
the restoring of a person to that condition from
which, contrary to right and duty, we have removed
him.

The reason for rendering satisfaction for our dishonesty is clear. The law of nature and the law of
the land affirm that every man ought to possess in
undisturbed use those goods to which he has a right.
If we steal something from our neighbor at nine
o'clock at night, it does not rightfully become ours at

ten o'clock. In other words, the passing of time does not change the right, nor make lawful that which was unlawful. Under the Levitical Law, the Jews were obliged to give "five oxen for an ox, and four sheep for a sheep." Time never cancels out the duty of restoring that which we have unjustly taken from another, regardless of how much sorrow we may have had for the theft. The proof that we are sorry is that we return the stolen goods.

To make money dishonestly and then put it in the wife's name is not to escape the obligation to make restitution. Since such a person never owned the property lawfully, he never could make the transfer legally. Suppose a man is sold a handkerchief on the pretense that it is silk, when really it is nylon— restitution must be made. A second-hand car dealer who tells a buyer that the car is in perfect condition, and yet knows that he filled the rear transmission with sawdust to hide for a hundred miles the defective gears—such a crook is bound to make restitution.

There is a story—and it is only a story—about a man who went to confession to a priest. During confession he stole the priest's watch. He then told the priest that he had stolen a watch. The priest said: "You must make restitution." The thief said: "I will give it to you, Father." "No," said the priest, "give it to the owner." The penitent said: "The owner won't take it back." "In that case," said the priest, "you can keep it."

If this were not a story, the penitent would still be bound to make restitution—not only to man but also to God. Honesty is not a policy; it is a duty!

Better than all the syllogisms of philosophers they prompt lives to nobler purposes and make them think of heavens. As there could never be a hero without danger, so there could not be tenderness without their helpfulness. Their loveliness substitutes joys for pleasure and makes us realize that all love ends in an incarnation—even the Love of God.

Children come to parents as so much plastic material and the shape that they take later on in life is to a great extent the responsibility of the parents themselves. When God sends a child into this world, He makes a little crown for it in Heaven, and woe to those parents who do not instruct their children and so make their own child a victim of Heavenly disinheritance. Every child is born close to Heaven's gate, which accounts for the readiness with which their affections so quickly turn to God when their parents do communicate the wonder of that love. Serious indeed it is to throw any impediment between them and their Saviour and to hold them back from being folded in the arms of His Grace. From this point of view children sometimes make parents feel very awkward, for how can parents teach them Divine Love unless they feel it themselves? The vine that will climb in June will be trained for Heaven's walls less aptly in the dry heat of the late summer.

No man can work well for the nation and the common good unless he is deeply rooted to a home. An engine cannot run a ship unless it is bolted to the hold. There is nothing that so much screws and bolts mankind to homes and to genuine patriotism as children. Before the father and the mother of the child were married, they often used to speak of the love that bound them together as "our love." They always referred to a third term outside of themselves as if to imply that they could not be bound together except by some strong arm which belonged to neither. When a child is born they begin to see concretized in visible form the embodiment of the mystery of their love. Like the love of earth and tree, their marriage becomes fruitful unto new love, as their two hearts conspire against their individual impotence, by filling up at the store of the other the lacking measure. And they build up not the mere sum of themselves but that new life which gives to the winter of marriage the springtime of fruit. Thus does marriage preserve its mystery and thus do husband and wife see that their love is a loan from the bank of life and is to be paid back into that bank with life and not with death.

If up to this point their love has been just an exchange of egotisms, they now feel all of their selfishness crushed and destroyed as they look out to that which their love mutually produced. The child of the human race, and the home becoming young again are therefore the hope of humanity.

daring was held to be loyal courage; prudent delay was the excuse of a coward; moderation was the disguise of unmanly weakness; frantic energy was the true quality of a man. The conspirator who wanted to be safe was a recreant in disguise; the lover of violence was always trusted and his opponent suspected."

The false principles behind this "feeling" theory of right and wrong are very evident: first, it is held that every experience is for its own sake, whether that experience be sexual, political, social or economic. The experience cannot be for the sake of anything else, there being nothing else but the self. Second, if we attempt to make any judgment on our experience, it must be done solely on the basis of whether or not the experience is pleasurable to the ego; if it makes me "feel good" it is right. Finally, since pleasure or thrill or utility is the sole standard of judgment, it follows the more intense the thrill, the more useful anything is to the self, the better it is.

In contrast with this position, compare what might be called the sensitiveness of innocence. The sensitiveness of innocence does not mean ignorance or "not having lived." Rather it is an awareness of what is good and true because one has avoided the false and the evil. The grammarian, who knows good style, is very sensitive to errors in writing or speaking; the physician is sensitive to disease and any deviation from the norm of health; the philosopher can detect at once a false reasoning process; the director of any orchestra, despite the number of musicians he has before him, can hear the false note from the smallest and least important of the instruments. So in the moral order, when Divine Innocence sat at table with a traitor, he said: "One of you is about to betray Me." Holiness can quickly detect blots.

The instinctive reaction of good children to evil is

not due to their rational immaturity, but to their maturity in innocence. Such judgments of innocence and purity are totally different from suspicion. Suspicion can often be a reflection of one's own failings. "Judge not and you will not be judged." Often, the sins we most loudly condemn in others, are those to which we are most secretly attached, or else constitute our greatest weakness. Purity is never suspicious but looks for some ground for reposing trust. It has a power of apprehension, a penetration, an insight, a talent for psychological discovery that comes not to those who have been infected by wrong. How often the judgment of a child in a family about a visitor is more correct than the judgment of the parents. Innocence made them detect a blemish which the less innocent failed to see. Grown-ups who have surrendered even the quest of goodness are often fearful of the innocence of children, not because they fear to contaminate them, but because they feel condemned unconsciously by the innocent. At the Last Supper when the Saviour said that "one" was about to betray, "all" asked: "Is it I?" No one can be sure of his goodness before innocence.

A society that needs healing and regeneration will receive it mostly from the innocent. The pure can look on the impure without contempt. It was Divine Innocence Who asked of a sinful woman: Where are they who accuse thee? There was no condemnation in Him Who was Righteousness itself; so there are sympathy and forgiveness and healing in the wings of the innocent.

CHAPTER TWENTY-FOUR

Forgiveness Not Enough

MODERN PSYCHOLOGY has deeply enriched our grasp
of the hidden motivations of the mind, but because
it has not taken guilt seriously, it has also missed one
of the major needs of the human heart, namely to
"make up" for the wrong that has been done. Most
boys, at one time or another, have broken windows;
those who had a training in honesty, not only sought
to recover that ball that went into the parlor, but also
to "pay for the window." This readiness to right a
wrong persists in adult life in most people where the
damage done is external, such as backing into a ga-
rage and breaking a door. But where there is moral
and inner guilt, such as excesses in alcoholism, car-
nality and slander, most people feel that all they have
to do is just "give up" the wrong and forget about it.

Even laws of physics suggest that this is not
enough. Picture a man standing at point A, which
represents a neutral zone. He is told by one whom
we will assume has the authority to command him,
to go three feet to his right. Suppose instead of obey-
ing, he goes three feet to his left. At that point,
realizing his disobedience, he asks for forgiveness and

receives it. But look where he is—three feet away from the neutral zone before he can go in the right direction. Before he can begin to go right, he must put his foot down three times in humble repentance as he previously had put it down three times in rebellion. A more simple example would be this: Suppose someone during a conversation steals your watch. He then has a remorse of conscience and asks your pardon which you readily grant. But the chances are you would also say: "But give me back my watch."

In addition then to being forgiven, some kind of amendment must be made for the offense. Every infringement of a law, whether civil or moral is a de-ordination. To restore balance and equilibrium, some compensation must be made. There is remorse in those who do wrong, but rarely any amendment. The thief is sorry that he is caught; the school teacher who sold out to the Reds is red-faced at being exposed, but this is not a renunciation of the evil which is proven real by "making up" for the betrayal. Money that is stolen must be paid back; slanders that were spread must be denied; secret sins must be wiped out by self-discipline and a mortification in proportion to the illegitimacy of the pleasure. It need not always be atoned for in the same kind, for "charity covers a multitude of sins." For that reason those who have been blessed with the world's goods can make reparation by helping the poor in God's name.

The psychological reason for the cruelty in the modern world is this: those who have a deep hidden sense of guilt, feel the need of making some reparation for it. But since they refuse to face their own moral guilt, they inflict on others a punishment which should have been inflicted on themselves. The man who is not hard on himself for his faults will always be hard on others. The proud man, who never admits he is wrong, loves to blame servants, golf clubs, the driver in "that car" and the Electra complex of his grandmother. The man who thinks he is not so bad never thinks of tearing little chunks off his ego in order to make himself the better character. The excessive cruelty of the Communists is due to this transfer of guilt from themselves to others.

When a man falls into sickness through excesses, the tenderness of the nurse and the doctor are apt to give him an excuse for a relapse. Unless he puts forth an equal effort to move to the opposite direction of his excesses, he will always remain their victim. The measure of our love for anything is the amount of pain we are willing to suffer to gain the object loved, or to avoid what is offensive and wrong.

The forgiveness of God is one thing, but the proof that we want that forgiveness is the energy we expend to make amends for the wrong. That is why through the tradition of all religions there have been several distinct types of retroactive amendment, such as prayer, fasting and alms. The stress that has been laid on these through the ages is a proof that time itself never blots out the offense. Suppose every time a man did wrong he was told to drive a nail into the wall; suppose every time he was forgiven the wrong, he was asked to take a nail out. The wall would not be clean and white; it would still be full of holes. It is the filling up of these holes that constitutes the clearing of the moral slate. When modern man recovers that attitude and begins to give to the poor and to be extra hard on himself in reparation for the wrong, then he will have taken his biggest step to that inner peace which not the world, but God alone gives.

CHAPTER TWENTY-FIVE

The Need of Self-Restraint

IF THERE IS any one lesson which our modern civilization finds it difficult to learn, it is the necessity of self-restraint. Education, advertising, and the general temper of the times allow the individual every pleasure he desires, and the fullest expression of his egotistic instincts. Communism fosters it by affirming that what is another's can become yours through violence. Socialism fosters it under the illusion that if the State does it for you, you really get it for nothing. Education pampers it by training the mind to absorb a few facts, to the utter forgetfulness of the training of the will, which is the seat of character.

The assumption is that we are so thoroughly good that any desire, libido, instinct, craving or appetite we have ought to be fulfilled. The truth is that there are also bad tendencies in us, and to the extent that we give way to them, we become their slave. This does not mean that our nature is wholly corrupt; it is not. It does mean, however, that like trains we can stay on the tracks laid down by the engineer, or else in false freedom get off them and "live our own lives." A river that stays within its bed can be the bearer of commerce, but a river that refuses to recognize limits becomes either a swamp or a flood. If there were not something in us which inclined us to evil, there would never be the insistence on mortification and penance which one finds in all religions. Neither would Christianity command: "Mortify your members."

The tendency to evil in us is like the law of gravitation which pulls us down to the animal; but there is another law of gravitation, which is spiritual, which urges us to seek the things that are above, particularly the fulness of Truth for our minds and the fulness of Love for our wills. There is a law in the mind and there is a law in the body, and sometimes they pull against each other, like a team of horses, one of which goes to the right and the other to the left. The mainspring of a watch when it is detached from its pivot does not stop immediately; but when uncontrolled it spins so rapidly as to ruin the mechanism. So we work well when controlled by the Law of God; but when we are in dis-harmony with what is best for our higher nature, we kill inner peace and happiness. There are a number of people in the world who are mental cases, or, in plain, old-fashioned language, crazy. But there are a number of people who have so often violated the laws of conscience and ruined the mechanism of their minds and hearts that they think they can be cured by the same therapy as the crazy people. This is impossible, because their trouble is in the moral order and not in the functional or organic order. They have ruined their lives by uncontrolled license, as a glass would ruin itself if used to break rocks.

Nobody likes to hear the word "sin" today, but we will begin to be happier when we realize that maybe most of our trouble comes from the fact that we are sinners. The need of alcohol and sleeping tablets are so many attempts to escape confronting ourselves with ourselves in the light of the moral law. Sin is de-ordination and in the broad sense of the term every de-ordination, if it is wilful and deliberate, is sin. Those who say that sin begets "a guilt complex" hope to scare the cure away by name calling. Is "a guilt complex" any worse than "an innocence complex" from which they suffer? Because a person is sick and asks for a physician, does he have "a sickness complex"?

Once one admits the plain fact that he has done wrong, he can be put on the right path by being shown that the same energy that he used to sin can now be diverted in the other direction. A sliver in a finger momentarily checks the circulation, but the blood flows on, trying to overcome the obstacle. This causes pressure, fever and congestion. The circulation is good, but here in this case it becomes an evil. So with sin. The action of our power and energies continues, but in the wrong direction. From this unholy marsh, poisonous gases arise that affect the mind. As a train that is derailed destroys itself by its speed, so does the man ruin himself who leaves the track of Divine Law. But, thanks to God's "grace and forgiveness," we can get back on the track and the same energy we used in the wreck can now be used to speed toward happiness. Sin is really power in reversed action, and the grace of God makes it flow in the right direction.

CHAPTER TWENTY-SIX

The Pharisee and the Publican

THE HEART that has sin in it, unless it repents, constantly has it coming out in criticism and hatred of others. Those who do not believe in the virtues of others betray viciousness in the depths of their own hearts. Those who accuse others of being actuated by self-interest are themselves selfish. It is always the crooked politicians who disbelieve in the honesty of decent politicians; thieves do not believe in the existence of honesty, and worldlings call religious people hypocrites because they know that if they expressed a warm regard for the things of God, they would be hypocrites.

What sin is to a soul, that an infection is to a body. Bad blood comes out in boils; bad morals come out in discontent, anxiety, slander and a thousand other signs of mental maladjustment.

It does no good to deny our moral lapses or to try to cover them up, as most people are trying to do today in busy-bodyism which sometimes goes by the name of "doing something for society." Our Lord told the story of two men who had hidden guilt; one the Pharisee who went to the front of the Temple and told God all he was doing to "make the world a better place to live in," how he helped the poor, rendered service to the government, and avoided all those public sins of which others are so often guilty. The mistake of the Pharisee was that he compared his life with the outward lives of disreputable people, and took to himself the credit of exalted superiority. It may be that the reason people like to hear and read of scandals is because they make them feel better than others. Hence the prayer: "I thank thee that I am not as the rest of men." There is a thrusting forward of the ego to which all else is made subservient, even the prayer and God.

When Philip, King of Macedonia, laid siege to the fair city of Samos, he told the citizens that he came a-wooing to it; but the orator of their country replied that it was not the fashion of his country to go a-wooing with fife and drum. So the Pharisee goes to the Temple a-wooing God with the exploits of his social action. It was his way of telling God that he had no need of Him, that he had no guilt to be forgiven, and no sin to be pardoned.

The Publican in the back of the Temple prayed: "Lord, be merciful to me a sinner." Against those who would say that redemption begins with fixation on guilt, it is here revealed that the true penitential spirit is born not so much by looking at our wickedness as at the Goodness of God; he who is sick and fixes his gaze on his sores rather than on the Physician is doomed to despair. It was not his sin that gave him the right to ask for mercy, but rather the Goodness of God. There is a balance between our misery and God's Mercy. If we concentrate on the Mercy of God, and debase not ourselves, we are apt to fall into presumption; if we debase ourselves and concentrate on our misery and forget the Mercy of

God we are apt to fall into despair. A God high in the heavens and the soul in the dust, such is the real combination that leads to newness of life. The higher a steeple rises in the heavens the smaller it becomes; the closer a saint gets to God the less he is in his own eyes. As John the Baptist said: "I must decrease, He must increase." The worst thing in the world is not sin; the worst thing is to deny that we have done wrong. The blind who deny that they are blind never will see; the lame who deny their disability never will walk.

The Pharisee in front of the Temple was typical of many of the modern psychological theories; it was based upon the idea of his own inner goodness. Many seem to be crying for madder and madder wine, louder and louder music, in order to drown out the voice of conscience that would make them Publicans humbly beating their breasts and asking pardon of God.

But when there is no longer a belief in the Goodness of God and the evil in our lives, the heart begins to sour. Whenever an age or a people become cynical about religion, there is hidden somewhere in souls a bitterness. Bitterness is an incentive to self-destruction. The man who is conscious of having done wrong beats his breast as did the Publican as if to pound out the evil in his heart. The cynic who has no God to Whom he can turn in his bitterness is apt to pound himself in suicide, for bitterness does end in self-destruction.

There is plenty of knowledge about the universe, but there is little of self-knowledge. People are frightened to look inside themselves. There are so many unwashed dishes in the sink of their consciences; their souls look like unmade beds. But if only once they would be humble enough to look inside and admit the mess, then look up to the Good and Merciful God like the Publican, they would see then how God "can write straight with our crooked lines."

HUMILITY

CHAPTER TWENTY-SEVEN

Humility

CERTAIN WORDS pass out of vocabulary until some incident or writer digs them up as forgotten treasures. One such word is "Humility." But often it happens that when words signifying great forgotten virtues are resurrected, they are used in an entirely new sense. For example, in China those who refuse to accept the domination of the Reds are accused of being wanting in "humility." The rat that rebels against being devoured by the mouse is also labelled as failing in that virtue.

Humility does not mean letting other people walk over you; humility is not passivity, submissiveness, nor underestimation of oneself; it is not condemnation, nor a belittling of oneself; it is not an enemy of greatness striving for the stars, for when God became man He gave the counsel: "Be ye perfect as your Heavenly Father is perfect." Humility is not a self-awareness that one is humble, for then it becomes pride; humility is not a self-contempt that prepares for gloom, or cynicism, nor is it believing that our talents are less valuable than they really are. A man six foot three who is praised for being so tall is not humble when he says: "Oh no, I am really only four feet four."

Humility is truth about ourselves; it is a virtue by which one does not esteem himself to be more than he really is. It therefore avoids an inordinate love of one's own excellence, and an inordinate pleasure in seeing others inferior to self. To see oneself as one really is, means that we must never mistake the imaginary self for the *real self*. The real self is what we are before God and before ourselves in an examination of conscience. Take an opera singer of undoubted excellence; she is not humble if she says: "Really, I can't sing a note." Rather her humility will consist in recognizing that she has received a tremendous endowment of a voice, and she will thank God for it. But the recognition of this truth must be counterbalanced by a recognition of her limitations. Because she thinks she is a good singer, she must not think she is necessarily a good acrobat. Humility holds her soul back lest she attempt the impossible. This is the great failing of those who have one talent. How often the scientist, because he knows experimental facts, is asked about a belief in immortality or belief in God— and with no humility parades as a master of all subjects because he is master of one.

Humility has a positive and a negative side. The positive side is living up to one's capacities and abilities—carpenters being good carpenters, baseball players being good baseball players, comedians being funny comedians, and physicists being good physicists. But humility in its negative side will keep them from overshooting their mark and morticians will not be comedians at funerals, theologians will not be scientists, and scientists will not be theologians. Humility then moderates our appetite for perfection, but it does not destroy it.

No man is humble who does not believe in God, and who does not recognize dependence on the Power that created him, the Love that redeemed him and the Spirit that sanctified him. Our imperfection in the face of God has its immediate compensation in the fact that God Who made us creatures will, with our cooperation, make us His children. Once humbled we become exalted, living no longer on the human level, but enjoying the glorious liberty of the children of God. In relation to neighbor, we look for the best that is in him, and for the worst that is in ourselves. This enables us to purge ourselves of our faults and to imitate the good qualities of our neighbor.

Children in a family without love become rebellious, recalcitrant, stubborn, selfish and cruel. Adults who live in a loveless or Godless world end in despair which is the last extreme of self-love. Those who are loved, become kind, ready for service and quick to love others. The humble man will then never be overcome by praise; he accepts praise to return it to God. *Fecit mihi magna, qui potens est, et sanctum nomen ejus.* "He Who is powerful has done great things for me and holy is His name."

CHAPTER TWENTY-EIGHT

Self-Inflation

ONE OF the celebrated portrait artists of the world once said that he never knew a person to sit for a portrait who did not constantly talk about himself. This may be explained psychologically as a desire to impress the artist with his greatness, in order that the artist might translate it onto the canvas. But it is more likely that the habit of egotism was already so deeply encrusted, that self praise was rather automatic; it showed itself in the Pullman car as well as in the studio. Rich men perhaps more than others, are the greatest boasters, though it may be unconscious. Confusing *having* with *being,* they think that since they possess material greatness, therefore, they must necessarily be great. Such proud people are much more subject to worry and anxiety than those who are not proud, for every little trial registers very sharply through their morbidly sensitive skin.

Nothing has so much contributed to egotism, pride, conceit, swell-headedness and braggadocio, as the assumption that an "inferiority complex" is always wrong. If the failure to assert oneself, to push others aside in seeking first places at table, is the mark of a psychic disease, then satanic pride is on the throne. Depreciation of the efforts of others, the swaggering playing out of a dream and an illusion, an excessive tenderness about any personal insults and a callousness toward the feeling of others, become the daily behavior pattern.

The egotist, standing alone in his self-imagined greatness, lives in a world of lie, because the truth about himself would puncture his self-inflation. Pride rightly has been called the source of all other evils. As the great poet put it, ''By that sin fell the angels; how can man then, the image of his Maker, expect to win by it?''

A word hardly ever mentioned in modern speech is ''Humility'' or the virtue which regulates a man's undue estimation of himself. Humility is not underestimating oneself, such as a talented singer denying that he can sing. Humility is truth, or seeing ourselves as we really are—not as we think we are, not as the public believe us to be, or as our press notices describe us. If the candle compares itself with the lightning bug, it boasts of the greater light; but if it compares itself with the sun, it sees itself but as its feeble ray. As the artist must judge his painting by the sitter, as the die maker must judge his coin by the model, so man must judge himself by His Maker and all that He intended man to be.

The humble man is not cast down by the censures or the slights of others. If he has unconsciously given occasion for them, he amends the faults; if he deserves them not, he treats them as trifles. Humility also prevents putting an extravagant value on the distinctions and honors. Praise will generally make him uncomfortable, because he knows that whatever talents he has, are gifts from God. He receives praise as the window receives light, not as the battery re-

ceives a current. The humble person may be a great
person, but if he possesses that virtue, he hires no
press agents, he blows no trumpets, he affects no
mannerisms, he unfolds no banners, he courts no
adulation, but while aiding and enlightening others,
he desires to be like the angels who, while ministering to others, are themselves unseen.

Humility is the pathway to knowledge. No scientist
would ever learn the secrets of the atom if, in his
conceit, he told the atom what he thought it ought to
do. Knowledge comes only with humility before the
object which can bring us truth.

In like manner, many minds today will not accept
Revelation or faith because their pride has blocked
the inflow of new knowledge. Only docile minds can
receive new truth. Pride makes a person insoluble
and, therefore, prevents his entering into amalgama-
tion with others. Humility, on the contrary, because
of its basic receptivity to the good of others, makes
it possible to receive the joys of union with God.
That is why Our Divine Lord suggested that uni-
versity professors will have to become children to
enter the kingdom of heaven; they must admit, like
children, that God knows more than they do.

"the cynic," as Oscar Wilde says, "is one who knows the price of everything and the value of nothing."

Judas had the money bag tied about his cincture while Mary broke the alabaster box. His criticism of her was born of his selfishness, as his avarice was related to his treason. He gave, however, a moral tone to his criticism by saying that the perfume could have been sold for three hundred pence and given to the poor. No one ever betrays the Divine or the virtuous without prefacing the betrayal by some false moral justification. Only half the soul is in the criticism, but Mary's whole soul was in the gift.

Few realize that criticism of others is often a betrayal of their own character. The reproach of Judas was based not on his love of the poor, but on the fact that he was a thief. For that reason, Our Divine Lord, Who knew the workings of every heart, said to Judas: "Leave her alone." A greeting without friendship in it, honeyed words without affection, pretended love of the proletariat without a right conscience—these are the false masks Our Lord would tear off the faces of critics. To value only what can be *"sold"* is to defile what is truly precious. The innocent joy of childhood, the devotedness of a wife, the self-sacrificing service of a daughter—none of these have an earthly market. To reduce everything to the dirty scales of economic values is to forget that some gifts, like Mary's, are so precious that the heart that offers them will be praised as long as time endures.

Because criticism can be disappointed ambition, it does not follow that it has no function. But it is well never to dig a hole unless you put something in it. Encouragement is often a better stimulus to improve efforts than any criticism. Our mood today is more critical than encouraging, perhaps because no one examines his own conscience, and few, therefore, are conscious of their own faults. There is no character in the world so bad that there is still not left within it a potency for betterment. A dry stick is better for burning than a wet stick, but there does come a moment when the flames can ignite it.

What human power cannot do, that Divine grace can do. Very likely Mary who broke the alabaster box was so criticized by her fellow creatures and finally by Judas that she came at last to realize the only refuge from the slings and arrows of critics is in the Heart that knows all and therefore can forgive all. Unhappy lives are already so filled with self-disgust that criticism only deepens their despair. We already have enough critics; now our poor world needs apostles of encouragement. But whence shall they come except from Hope born of a Loving and Merciful Saviour?

CHAPTER THIRTY

Crutch or Cross

THE OTHER DAY a husband who admitted he could not be faithful to his wife, upbraided her for turning to God, saying that she was using religion as a crutch. The assumption behind such a statement is that one ought to live on his own moral fat and be dependent on nothing outside oneself. The rotten luxury of living on and for one's own ego is here exalted to a point where the eye is called a crutch because it leans on the birds and flowers for seeing; the ear is called a crutch because it leans on the song of the birds and the sigh of the waterfall for hearing; the stomach is labelled a crutch, but it craves food.

Nothing in nature is complete within itself; everything looks to something outside and beyond self except the egotist. The glory of the clouds is to die in showers, spending themselves on others. But the egotist, living only for self, must eventually fall into despair and unhappiness when he discovers his own bankruptcy. Once all the honeyed treasure of his body is spent, with no new life to show, then he discovers the lonesomeness of being alone.

Religion is actually not a crutch; it is a cross. It

is not an escape, it is a burden; not a flight, but a response. We speak here of a religion with teeth in it, the wind that demands self-sacrifice and surrender. One leans on a crutch, but a cross rests on us. A coward can use a crutch, but it takes a hero to embrace a cross.

Let him who thinks the cross is easy admit that he is wrong, or that he has broken a relationship of love, and then strive to right the wrong by penance and self-discipline, and he will discover the courage it takes.

The cross is laid on the shoulders of our pride and envy, our lusts and our angers, until by its friction it wears them away, and thus brings us to the great abiding joys of life. Like a canary, the best songs are learned in darkness. A canary will learn only snatches of song while there is light in the cage, but in darkness it learns the song until its heart is so full of it that it never forgets.

The springs of fresh water well up amid the brine of the salt sea; the fairest Alpine flowers bloom in the most rugged mountain passes; and the noblest songs were the outcome of the profoundest agony of soul. No one would say that the gold leans on the crutch of fire when it is purified of its dross; nor that the marble leans on the crutch of the chisel as the hidden form is revealed. Alcoholism is the crutch of a man who cannot live with his own conscience; religion is the cross of a man who purifies his conscience and no longer needs the drug.

When the mother asked Our Lord that her two sons be placed at the right and left side of Him in His glory, she actually asked for two crutches. But Our Lord asked in return if they could drink of the chalice of self-forgetfulness and moral heroism. As snow is cold and yet warms and refreshes the earth,

so afflictions and efforts at moral regeneration warm
and perfect the soul. The crutch-leaners rot in
honey; the cross-bearers are preserved in brine. After
a forest fire has raged furiously, it is discovered that
the seed of some of the pine cones have been re-
leased by the heat; so too taking up the cross has
been the condition of making souls first happy and
then saints.

The escapists who call religion a crutch are like
the blind who call those who see visionaries. A
boat is not a crutch to a man who wishes to cross
the river, nor is a pencil a crutch to a hand that
wants to write. But the man who has not brains
enough to write, or has not courage enough to learn
will call the pencil a "crutch." The heroes must be
prepared for the mockery of the weak. Once the Divine Hero was flung on His Cross the crutch-callers
asked Him to come down. They knew that that kind
of love was the death of self-love. Ever since the
world has been divided between those who call religion a crutch because, being lame, they think everyone else is lame, and those who called religion a cross
and believe—"Take up your cross daily and follow
Me."

CHAPTER THIRTY-ONE

Religion Not Popular

ALMOST EVERYONE today wants religion, but everyone wants a religion that does not cost too much; that is why Christianity has been watered down to suit the modern mind. Everyone wants good health, but not everyone believes in dieting or giving up things which are bad for the organism; in like manner, many have a vague aspiration for goodness without the will to implement it with sacrifice. The tens of thousands who in the past year have tried to give up smoking cigarettes, and then, after twenty-four hours, saw their resolution go up in smoke, can testify how little the modern mind is prepared for any kind of real sacrifice or self-denial.

It is not easy to say "No" to oneself; that is why so many philosophers have erected a philosophy of life based on saying "Yes" to every impulse and desire while dignifying it with the name "self-expression." But the fact still remains that serious progress in every walk of life demands some form of restraint; the doctor, the lawyer, the athlete, the artist, the singer, the businessman must all learn to "scorn delights and live laborious days" if they are to attain their ideals. The expert in Oriental languages or archeology cannot at the same time be a champion tennis player. In all walks of life, something must be sacrificed if something is to be gained; the mind is developed at the expense of the body, and the body at the expense of the mind.

Religion starts with an emptying of self. The Spirit cannot come into the soul until the ego begins to hang outside its tinsel dwelling the sign: "Immediate Occupancy." The ego or the selfish part of existence has to be broken like the shell of an egg, before there can be the development of the personality which at the beginning is as helpless as a chick. But because the ego does not wish to be tamed and disciplined, it flatters itself that mortification is the "destruction of personality" and thus prepares for its own stagnation.

Detachment from certain things is essential for attachment to God, just as the attachment of a husband to a wife demands detachment from other women. As Thomas Aquinas said: *"Man's heart adheres the more intensely to one thing, the more it is withdrawn from others."* The human heart is like a stream which loses depth as it divides its waters of affection into many channels. A true patriot cannot serve several countries, and a truly religious man cannot serve both God and Mammon. Hence, Our Lord gave the injunction: *"Take up your cross daily and follow Me."* First it is to be noted that the cross is personal. Most of us are willing to take up our own, or custom-built crosses; those that we have fitted to our own shoulders; but few there are who, like the Saviour, are willing to take the cross that is handed to them.

It is the trials imposed upon us by others, such as their injustices, their harsh words, their knife-in-the-back attitudes, and their peevishness, that gall us; yet these are counted as the daily crosses of the man who would be truly religious. Much of the weariness of the spiritual life is due to the constant necessity of bearing the shortcomings of others, along with the never ending strife against our own base inclinations. When other people begin "to get on our nerves," one must ask oneself if it is because they cross our moods or our wishes; in that case, it is self-will in us that adds to the weight of the cross.

Then begins the task of accepting such people as a cross, and through our patience and forgiveness, putting love where we do not find it. How many people there are in Church on Sunday sitting in the first seat of the pew, who resent anyone asking them to "please move over." They came to kneel before a cross, but they do not want one standing alongside them. How many there are too who sing lustily the hymn:

> *"Were the whole realm of nature mine,*
> *That were an offering far too small."*

and then, when the collection box is passed, they drop in a nickel. The fact is religion is popular only when it ceases to be truly religious. Religion by its very nature is unpopular—certainly unpopular with the ego.

CHAPTER THIRTY-TWO

Inner Nakedness

AN ETERNALLY FEMININE problem is always: "What will I wear?" It probably began the day after the initial rebellion, when Eve looked up at the leaves on the fig tree and said: "I wonder which one I will wear today?" Or it may have been that she turned to Adam and said: "I haven't a stitch to my name." In any case, it is interesting to note that in the account of the Fall, given in the Book of Genesis, Adam and Eve were not conscious of the need of clothes until after they had sinned. Very likely there had been an effulgence of their soul shining through their bodies which became as garments of radiance. Perhaps the glory attendant upon Christ on the Mountain of the Transfiguration was His Divinity shining through His humanity. So, too, the inner holiness of our First Parents was in a certain sense their garment not made with hands. After that inner beauty of the soul was lost, there was need of outer clothing. Once naked on the inside, external covering was necessary. Clothed originally with grace and holiness, there was no sense of nakedness, either inside or out.

Modern psychology has recovered this truth hidden

in the First Book of the Bible. Its expression of the truth is that excessive luxury on the outside is often a sign of nothing on the inside. "Defensive mechanisms" are attempts to hide some failing, defect or spiritual nakedness. For example, a young woman who wants to appear learned will cultivate an accent, use the jargon of the intelligentsia, and begin conversations with: "Oh, you never read Professor Schlamz' book on 'The Subaltern Relationship of the Id to the Sex-Libido in the Introverted Schizophrenics'?" How often, too, the man who has made a lot of money, either through oil spouting in his face or through unearned increment in real estate, will try to cover up his ignorance or his intellectual nakedness by considering all talk except money as a "waste of time."

This love of display to hide moral and spiritual nudity thus manifests itself in negative fashion. College students seeking to make up for a want of recognition, will seek to attract attention by wearing loud clothes. Bad clothes, baggy and misfitting garments will sometimes be worn to solicit the eyes of others. This is an old trick. Centuries ago, Plato, a man of taste who had fine carpets in his home, was visited by Diogenes, who lived in a tub and said disagreeable things about others because they were not as poor as he. One day, Diogenes, in an ill temper, came to visit Plato and, stamping on the carpets, said: "I trample on the pride of Plato." "Yes," said Plato, "and with greater pride."

The soul has its apparel as well as the body, and the psychologists are right in saying that exaggerated display on the outside is a sign of barrenness within. The external first meets the eye, and there is a natural tendency to judge the contents by the wrappings; diamonds wrapped in a newspaper clipping

SORROW

CHAPTER THIRTY-THREE

Mystery of Suffering

GOD BREATHES on man in his joys; He whispers in his conscience; He speaks in his troubles, and He shouts in his pains. Suffering is too great a mystery for reason to fully comprehend its meaning; its understanding demands a loftiness of soul and surrender of spirit which few are prepared to make.

Pain and suffering seem to be closely linked up with the cosmos itself, as if by some great free decision on the part of man the peace and concord of life were disturbed. Our solar system itself began with some great travail and labor of a major disturbance; our own planet had its ice age, with great waters vomiting themselves through hills and mountains, and our earth has its tumultuous change of seasons.

When we come to man, there are two kinds of sufferings: the pure and the impure. The impure pains are those which come from without through no fault of our own, such as plagues, disease, accidents, etc. Pure pain is that which comes from ourselves, such as physical pains resulting from an abuse of the laws of health: excesses in drinking, or worries, fear, anxieties caused by violation of the moral law.

It must never be thought that, because one suffers, therefore one is guilty or is being punished. In a general way, the disorders and evils of the world do follow from man planting a rebel's flag against the Creator; but it can never be said in any individual case the suffering was due to personal guilt. The Christ Who died on the Cross did nothing wrong. Innocence can suffer as well as the guilty.

More important is the question: what can one do in the face of pain and suffering? Various solutions have been offered. One is Stoicism, which is to grit one's teeth and bear it, in order to prove apathy and indifference to the ills of the world; another way is that of Buddhism, which is to see all suffering as the result of desire. As one crushes desire and strives for union with the great Nirvana of unconsciousness, one diminishes and finally conquers suffering. The Old Testament, as revealed in the Book of Job, is to acknowledge that we are face to face with a mystery which is incapable of solution by reason. When Job asks God questions, God appears and begins asking Job questions, such as, "Where were thou when I laid the foundations of the earth?" When God finished asking Job questions, Job realized that the questions of God made more sense than the answers of men. Job's final philosophy was summed up in "I will trust Him, though He slay me."

The Christian answer is that evil is due basically to sin. Hence the way to conquer suffering is to conquer sin. To do so, the Son of God took on Himself a human nature. Identifying Himself with man, He took on also His guilt as a father takes on the debts of a wayward son. Being man, He could suffer as man, and in the name of man; being God, His sufferings would have infinite value, and blot out all the debts against man. The Resurrection was the final manifestation that love of God is stronger than the power of sin. If pain and suffering were insoluble, the Heavenly Father would never have fitted it into the pattern of His Divine Son.

The lesson is that perfection is attained through work, sacrifice and self-denial. Sometimes it is self-imposed, and at other times imposed by others; then it becomes necessary to patiently bear the Cross in love of Him Who died for us. A mother gives a child bitter medicine; though the child protests, he knows it comes from a loving hand and for his own good. Love cannot extinguish suffering, but it can diminish it, as love makes an all-night vigil by her sick child seem less hard. Where there is this assurance that love suffered for us to atone for our sins, we can find peace in resigning ourselves to the Divine Will. As Dante said: "In Thy Will, O Lord, is our peace." Franz Werfel, continuing that idea, gave this motto to Peacemakers: "Not revenge, but expiation; not punishment, but penance."

CHAPTER THIRTY-FOUR

Sorrow and Anguish

GOD made this world too small for us! Our desires are greater than our realizations; our dreams are sweeter than life, and our hopes vaster than our loves. We have an ocean of desires, but only a cup with which to dip into the vast expanse. Each moment we bump into the walls of the universe and skin our shins on its fences. This is the basic cause of all yearning and all suffering. We were made for the infinite. We have wings on our soul but we beat them against the cage of our body and the triviality of our cities.

The first response of all religion to the torment of the soul is that we were made for God. If we already had it in our soul to love God for whom we were made, there would never need to be any sorrow. Sorrow to some extent supplies the deficiencies of our love. We often learn to love the law that fingers should not be stuck on a fire by having our fingers burned. A loving obedience to our parents would save us from the disaster, but where love failed, pain slipped in to teach us the needed lesson. Made for God, we bury ourselves in the trinkets of earth as if made only for them. We build our nest in the earth, hoping we can find contentment there and yet sorrow comes like a firebrand to burn it. As pleasures satiate, as our body gets fed up with thrills, as friends forget, and as power makes us uneasy, we say more and more in our heart of hearts, "Oh God, does everything pass but Thee?"

The mission of sorrow is not only to remind us that this earth is not all, but also to help expiate and atone for our sins. Sorrow is placed near evil to help redeem the soul. Thus sorrow need not always be *external,* such as sickness or accident; it can be, and most of it is, *internal*—a *malaise,* a discontent, a gnawing of conscience, a feeling that all is not right, an emptiness and a loneliness. It is the latter kind of sorrow that is drawing many hearts and souls today back again to God. Nothing so much wants a heart to be filled as a deep thirst. It was under this analogy that Our Saviour converted the woman at the well. She already had five husbands and the man with whom she was living was not her husband. And yet she thirsted for love. It is also interesting that she is the first one in Scripture to apply to Him the term "Saviour of the world." And what He saved her from was emptiness and thirst.

This latter quality of thirst might be called anguish rather than sorrow. Everyone suffers from anguish, even youths in the midst of their joys. Anguish is in some way related to hope, a feeling that the universe is not vain and that the aspiration of the soul ought to be satisfied somewhere. Pessimism looks to the past which it believes cannot be redeemed, but anguish looks to the future, with a hope that the past can be undone. Anguish comes too from a realization that one has powers that have never been used, and this makes the soul look out to a higher realm where they can be summoned to exercise and action. Anguish is not born of weakness, but of strength and possibility, just as sorrow is born of limitations.

Modern man, instead of being driven to despair, can begin to hope, for in anguish God is urging the soul on to a love that lies beyond all love, and a "Beauty that leaves all other beauty pain." It is the peculiar quality of this century which has amassed more wealth and power than any other century, to be also the century of greatest anguish. Those who regard this emptiness like that of a canyon fall into despair and darkness; those who see in it the emptiness of a reed can pipe the tunes of the Infinite and be made merry with the song.

COMMUNICATION

CHAPTER THIRTY-FIVE

Reading

WITHIN THE PAST YEAR the non-fiction books surpassed in sales fiction or novels. This is a happy trend in our contemporary civilization, for the reader of a serious book must always keep an active mind, whereas the reader of fiction may be passive and accept the doings and the musings of the characters as they are unfolded. It is interesting to make a comparison of the book reviews in the London Times Literary Supplement and the book reviews in many of our leading newspapers. Just for the fun of it, we counted the number of novels reviewed in one of the book-review sections of an American newspaper, and found 25 were reviewed in one issue; counting as non-fiction everything that was not a novel, there were only 13 serious books reviewed. Turning to the London Times Literary Supplement, we counted 9 novels reviewed, as compared with 40 works of non-fiction. The novel has value and ofttimes can present a moral or economic problem in the concrete far better than can be done in the abstract writing of non-fiction.

While each person is entitled to his preferences, the fact still remains that for the complete development of the mind, there must be serious and intelligent reading—not just reading. A king of Poland in the eighteenth century, speaking of those who read too much and absorbed too little, reflected: "A well-read fool is the most pestilent of blockheads; his learning is a flail which he knows not how to handle, and with which he breaks his neighbor's shins as well as his own." As the stomach can suffer from indigestion, so can the mind. If too many ideas are poured into it and there are not sufficient juices of the intellect to absorb them, a queer kind of literary constipation follows. As Milton said, one can be "deep versed in books and shallow in himself."

Not long ago, we were talking to a young college student who boasted of his vast reading, and said that Freud developed the idea of the inferiority complex. When it was suggested that possibly he was confusing Freud with Adler, his remark was: "Well, I ought to know, I visited Vienna and that is where Freud lived." Many people live under the illusion that they have read more than they actually have. There is hardly anyone who has been through college, who does not live under the false belief that he has had Darwin's "Origin of Species" or Spenser's "Faerie Queene." It has been said that some of the great geniuses of the past never read half as much as the mediocre geniuses today, but what they read they understood and incorporated into a deeper dimension of knowledge.

There is a world of difference between a mind that has in it ten thousand bits of uncorrelated information, and a mind that is like an organism in which one fact or truth is functionally related to every other truth, as the heart is related to the legs and arms. The wisest of men read out of a philosophy of life, as he eats out of a philosophy of health. Mental garbage is as scrupulously avoided by the eyes in reading, as another kind of garbage is avoided by the lips. On the other hand, certain "hard" reading, such as Plato, Aquinas, Toynbee, pass like iron in the blood and into the mind, giving it consistency and strength.

The easiness with which reading matter can be procured today has much to do with the ministering of lower tastes. Those who had a taste for philosophy in the days of Aristotle, a yearning for poetry in the days of Dante, for metaphysics in the days of Abelard, and for sacred science when the monasteries held all the treasures of knowledge—spared no effort to absorb learning. But now that reading is accessible in every drugstore and city corner, the discrimination has decreased with the availability.

After a time, useless reading weakens the mind rather than strengthens it; then reading becomes an excuse for the mind to lie dormant while thoughts are poured over it like chocolate over ice cream. The mind is like an hourglass through which ideas pass like sands, nothing remaining. The modern man has more leisure than the men of a century ago, but he knows less what to do with it. Our education is rightly preparing us to make a living. But let education not forget that since man has more leisure than working hours, it might teach him how to spend his leisure. Give a man a taste for the intellectual, the

CHAPTER THIRTY-SIX

How to Read

NEVER BEFORE in the history of the world were human eyes presented with more written words than in this our confused hour. A century ago it was believed that print would make everyone wise and good, just as food makes a man healthy. But food can produce gout, and print can also produce intellectual indigestion. Because of the abundance of words offered to the public it might be helpful to ponder a few suggestions on the subject of reading—serious reading.

In French, the word to read is *lire;* the word for choose or select is *elire*. The first rule then is: the best way to *lire* is to *elire*. Books, magazines and papers are like the multitudes of people we meet in the subway, the ball park, cocktail lounges and county fairs. We cannot possibly make all of them our companions, so we make a selection. Out of the crowd of books which push and shove themselves under our eyes, we have to select and extract those few which are fit to be our companions. As a bee makes honey only from a small part of the mass of the flower, so the mind acquires truth only from a fraction of that which is stamped out on a linotype machine. A negative way of stating the rule is to eliminate that which is non-essential and which is incapable of nourishing the mind.

But that brings up the question: But how choose? The second rule answers this question in the negative: Do not make it a rule only to read what is ''just out'' or the ''book of the week.'' This does not mean that these are to be excluded, but rather that it is not good for the mind to be guided by the principle that the latest is necessarily the best: What better proof is there of this than the fact that nothing seems as old to us today as the book that was on the best selling list three years ago; it seems almost as old and as antiquated as yesterday's newspaper. Nothing is a better eliminator of the chaff from the wheat than time; in its own silent way it swings the scythe and cuts down the mediocre and the highly advertised. It is not nearly as important to read what is just off the press as it is to read something that needed to be reprinted after a lapse of time. A classic, such as the Sonnets of Shakespeare, means something that has survived time and, therefore, is worthwhile.

A third rule is to avoid those books which excite emotions but never lead to action. Some books excite emotions and inspire action. These are to be cultivated for they produce an intimate communion with what we read. Such was the effect of a book of Cicero on Augustine and the treatises on Aristotle by Aquinas. Such emotions are good because they increase our understanding of life, deepen our desire to do good, enlighten our pathways and above all spur us to further action. Any book which inspires us to lead a better life is a good book.

But there are other emotions which are divorced entirely from action, truth and goodness, for example, a sentimental love story, a melodrama about a fiend with poison. Emotions of fear, love, justice, revenge, are provoked by what is read, but they never lead anywhere; they are passions without deeds, feelings without action. After a while, our heart becomes like the spring on a screen door with which a child plays by opening and closing it. . . . "just for fun."

The spring loses all its resiliency and eventually refuses to function. How many have emotions aroused without an appropriate object on which to operate; their emotion of love is aroused, but it is only to a nonexistent character; their emotion of rage against injustice is enkindled but it burns out on a page. Such minds become like stomachs that emit gastric juices at the sight of food but never are given anything to eat. One of the reasons why so many are left cold at the cruel injustices of the world, and are unmoved by the multiplied tragedies, is because their emotions are already jaded and worn. When an object is presented on which the emotions ought to play, they are incapable of acting. If the time is shorter than we think, then it behooves man to read well by choosing well.

CHAPTER THIRTY-SEVEN

Controlled Speech

SOME people say that their heads are right on top of their stomachs, and when anything goes wrong with their stomachs they cannot sleep. An equally serious condition is one in which words are always on the tips of people's tongues, so that reason never intervenes to stop their utterances. This advice was once given to those whose speech is intemperate: "Think before you speak; then talk to yourself." Ruling the tongue is one of the most difficult of all tasks. For that reason the ancient Persians taught their youths two things: to be secret, and to tell the truth.

Those who abuse speech are divided into three general classes: The first are those who are always "putting people in their place" as if they were ordained by God and the Constitution to "tell off" everybody for what they call "their own good." The second class is made up of those who detract from the merit of others by criticizing, finding fault or putting an evil interpretation on all they say or do. They go to an art museum and criticize every picture for not being hung properly, but they can never see that the pictures in their own homes are all upside down. A critical spirit is born of wrong behavior. There is not a critical person in the world who is not in need of criticism. Criticism of others is an escape from necessary self-criticism. The third class is made up of just plain liars. Conscious of their own littleness and insignificance, they try to give weight to their characters by exaggeration, or by creating a mythical world which is built according to their own specifications.

Socrates said: "Speak that I may see thee." Speech is the index of the mind and the summation of a soul, all that the person has been, is, and will be. We need only hear a word and we can say: "He is an ignorant man," "he is a proud man," "he is a kind man," "he is a cruel man." The whirlwind on the tongue is the sign of the tempest in the soul. If there is envy in the heart, it will show in the tone of the voice; if there is love in the heart even the words share the glow. But a skunk in the cellar soon smells up the whole house. It is a physical and psychological impossibility to develop the art of conversation without first developing the art of a good and humble heart out of which come our words. The power of edifying speech increases with the improvement in morals. Many of the suggestions offered today for the refinement of the art of conversation are in reality nothing else than the art of deceit and amount to "How to disguise your feelings," "How to praise when you want to damn," "How to compliment when you want to condemn," "How to influence people when you hate them."

Words are to be judged in two ways: by their transparency and by their purpose. Words should be like windows: We should be able to see through them.

They should not be like curtains which veil the inside of the mind from the outside of the lips. An equal sign should always be made between what is in the mind and what is on the lips; if we cannot make the equation, the words should not be said. There is hardly a human who has not at some moment of life come face to face with persons who never said what they meant, or never meant what they said. Many others, on the contrary, so spoke that the words were like open doors to their hearts. If they invited you to dinner, they really meant it.

Speech also has morality. Speech is a vehicle for the transportation of ideas, as an automobile is a vehicle for the transportation of persons or things. We judge the morality of a vehicle by the purpose for which it was made. An automobile used to rob a bank is the wrong use of a vehicle; words used to deceive, to malign, to destroy character are for that reason unmoral. A Communist who uses freedom of speech to destroy freedom of speech has used the vehicle of words for an evil purpose, and is to be judged in exactly the same way as a motorist who uses his car to run down pedestrians.

The horse has a bit, the ship a rudder, and man has a mind made to control his words. This applies equally to men and women through their conversations. Men generally speak about things; women generally speak about persons. The women used to be called the gossips. Now that dubious honor is being stolen by the men. When a patient goes to see a doctor he says: "Let me see your tongue." We have a Divine assurance that something like that will be said by the Divine Physician on the last day. He said that we would be held responsible for every idle word. Conscious of that responsibility, it helps to keep in mind the words of David: *"I will take heed to my ways, that I offend not with my tongue; I will keep my mouth with a bridle, when the wicked is beside me."*

TWO FAMOUS CLASSICS OF SPIRITUAL WISDOM
BY BISHOP FULTON J. SHEEN

Way to Happiness
D473

Way to Inner Peace
D474

No man today is more eminently qualified to answer questions about the meaning of life than Fulton J. Sheen. His words have a meaning for everyone regardless of religion or creed. *Way to Happiness* and *Way to Inner Peace* are inspirational blueprints for everyone who seeks a richer, more satisfying way of life.

TRULY INSPIRING BOOKS
BY A TRULY INSPIRED MAN

ONLY 50¢ EACH

WHEREVER PAPERBACKS ARE SOLD

A Fawcett Crest *Reprint*

FAWCETT WORLD LIBRARY

If your dealer is sold out, send cover price plus 10¢ each for postage and handling to Crest Books, Fawcett Publications, Inc., Greenwich, Conn. If order is for five or more books, no postage or handling charge is necessary. Order by number and title. No Canadian orders.